"Ignorance is the curse of God;
knowledge is the wing
wherewith we fly to heaven."
(William Shakespeare)

Mihály Tóth

KNOWLEDGE COMMERCE MILLIONAIRE

BUILD YOUR PROFITABLE CONSULTING, EXPERT OR COACHING BUSINESS BY SHARING YOUR KNOWLEDGE.

THE GROWTH OF "KNOWLEDGE COMMERCE" IS UNSTOPPABLE. IT PRODUCES AN AVARAGE $27.739.726 INCOME PER HOUR AND WITHIN THE FOLLOWING 6 YEARS 300% OF INCREASE CAN BE EXPECTED BY SHARING KNOWLEDGE.

Author : Mihály Tóth

FIRST EDITION

Copyright. All rights reserved.

The book – without the written consent of the author– cannot be copied or conveyable, neither on the whole nor in parts, in any form or sense, neither in an electronic form nor in a mechanic way including public presentation or courses, audio book, any kind of appearance on the internet, in xerox, as a recording or any form of information record.

Copyright owner: © Tóth Mihály, 2020

Appointed publisher:

www.knowledgecommercemillionaire.com

You are lucky to be able to be reading this…

The world is changing and knowledge is going to be the highest value worldwide.

Information in itself is not enough anymore, but if information is combined with experience and wisdom, it becomes applicable knowledge.

The most powerful currency of the future will be KNOWLEDGE and whoever possesses knowledge, will also have the benefits. The most successful future entrepreneurs will be those who share their knowledge with others.

Imagine, to how many people you can give value by sharing your knowledge with them that you had gained in 10 years of being able to play the guitar. Make an online guitar course and sell it to thousands of people. This is going to be the best WIN-WIN deal business as your client purchases valuable knowledge at a competitive price as well as you will be able to help thousands by doing this. If 1000 clients pay you $100 in the first year then you can achieve $100.000 income by investing the same amount of energy and work.

This book will transform your mindset and will encourage you to build your own, new business and to be among the firsts building knowledge based online business.

Michael Tóth
Wien, Austria
2020.10.01.

Anyone can become a Digital Millionaire

First of all, I would like to clarify the meaning of „Knowledge Commerce" and that is why it is going to be so important to you in the future. Most people start businesses in which they have to invest enormous amount of money and to have the return on their investments will take between 5-10 years.

Knowledge Commerce is much simpler than that and you can start it with only few assets and become successful easily. This is a business where the value is the knowledge in your head. The good news is that it cannot be stolen or copied by anyone.

Even those who are currently staring helplessly and say: „ I do not have any outstanding knowledge" can build a 100 million dollar business.

I wrote this book to help you in finding the knowledge you can build upon your knowledge based business. With the help of this book you will reach a $10.000 income in the first year already.

Does it sound good? Then let's get it started.

Are you ready to generate $100.000 income from your knowledge annually? The target is 100K monthly. LET'S GO.

Now read the book, make notes or even doodle it. Use the book and do not let it get dusty. Everything is in it that you need to know, so that way it is only up to you whether you make the best business of your life or not.

0.) Introduction to the Online Expert Business	15
How do you recognize a Digital Millionaire?	17
How to use this book efficienly?	27
Who is Michael Tóth and why to trust Him?	29
Can someone become a Digital Millionaire who is not an expert?	32
1.) How to become a well-paid expert?	39
It does not matter if you are not a trained professinal with a university degree	39
Self-development + Practice = VALUABLE KNOWLEDGE	42
Build positive and fruitful relationships	47
Ask what their problem is and offer a solution	50
Consider money as a power source and invest it	53
Dare to dream big. Thousands of customers are waiting for you	58
2.) Let's plan your expert business	63
The 6 greatest advantages of the expert business	65
The 10 steps expert business building formula	71
Expert values that you must acquire	77
The 6 pillars of the expert business	80
Building expert product funnel	84
1# Create your free lead magnet	89
2# Plan your initial product offer	95
3# Your irrefutable main product offer	98
4# Let's maximize your profit by further offers	100

5# Let's plan your $20,000 income per month	104
3.) The toolkit of digital millionaires	**110**
What kind of tools are you going to need?	110
Which microphone should I choose for making the video?	113
What type of camera should I use for recording the video?	115
Natural light or softbox? Which one you should choose.	118
5 softwares that helped me build my own business	121
Presentation softwares for making presentations	125
Kajabi : The heart and soul of your online business	128
4.) Let's plan your first online course	**136**
The strategical and thematic planning of an online course	136
Scheduling the course and creating the layout of the presentations	139
What do you need when you are making the course?	142
5.) Let's sell your online course	**150**
Make your own irrecusible offer	150
Goal => Strategy => Tactics => Daily tasks	154
Try Kajabi software for free	157

0.) Introduction to the

Online Expert Business

0.) Introduction to the Online Expert Business

Dear Reader,

I am grateful that you have bought my book. This is the introductory chapter in which I would like to present you the lifestyle you can achieve with my assistance.

Before I start writing about the many positive things, I would like to make it clear that this book in not a printed training material to become a millionaire as you will not become a millionaire by merely reading it.

You have to work hard to make yourself known by your potential customers. You will feel many times that your days merge and you do not have weekends but you will proceed and build your business.

It does not matter if you push on work day and night as that way you will shortcut the way to success.

Every step, tool and technique is included in this book which enables you to build your own expert online business that will make you millions.

Read the book, make notes and complete the workbook.

Follow my instructions and I guarantee you that within a couple of months you will see the progress in yourself and in your bank account.

Have a great progress and a fast increasing bank account.

Best wishes,

Mihály Tóth.

How Do You Recognize a Digital Millionaire?

We are different from those parvenus who obtained their wealth by tricking, connections or inheritance.

We can always create value. You can deprive a digital millionaire from everything he or she has, but his or her knowledge and list of contacts and within just one year he or she will strive himself or herself back to the same level as he or she had been before.

Nevertheless, there is one thing that differentiates us from each and every millionaire. This is: our mindset. We think differently therefore we are capable of achieving greater things. We, digital millionaires know how to produce efficiently and we deal with our money more wisely. We do not prodigalize our money on luxury products and lavish cars, but rather invest it willfully in developments and profit making marketing campaigns.

We do not wear expensive outfits, we drive average cars and many times we would not even be rated as middle-class. In shops, we pay careful attention on what we buy and whenever we can we save money as it means a power resource to us.

The profit we make is a little, streaming brook that will grow into a river if we let it grow.

The more money we can save the more we can invest in our expert businesses. By doing this, you can save years and become a market leader in your own field within months, even if it seems incredible for you now.

You know, if I was able to do it, then you can also do it.

Story: How much do you earn while you ski?
We live in Austria close to Vienna and my favorite ski resort is approximately one and a half hour away. In winter, when the ski season starts, I work one or two days a week, and the rest of the days I go skiing. From December to April we can bump into each other with a great chance on the ski tracks because I can be found really often. I can afford it because working one or two days a week is enough for recording videos or writing texts and set automated processes.

While skiing I follow the notifications and it is a fantastic feeling to see when a $1.000 purchase comes in on a day when I am on the piste the whole day and I slack.

It happened to me in the ski season of 2019 that I bumped into a ski instructor, who trained young boys between the age of 6 and 10. I asked him how his job was, what kind of qualification was needed to be certified to be able do it and how much could be earned by doing it as a job. I also talked about my own automated business, and in the end, I got a weird question that I have to share with you:

„How much do you earn this way during skiing?"

The answer was surprising for him… I took my mobile phone and checked the amount of income that I reached for that day through Stripe application. The $1.350 daily income was clearly visible on the screen. This is completely passive income, which means that I do not have to do anything as the automated system withdraws the money and provides access to my courses.

„This is really good, but I think only few can achieve it."

Yes, but it has a reason. Most coaches, consultants and experts do not know those techniques and tools by which this system can be built. Excellent professionals, but they are not familiar with marketing and automatization.

After the short but exciting conversation I went to have lunch and my mind was working meanwhile. Unfortunately, many people do not know how to use these systems. How should I help them?

How could I help 100.000 coaches, experts or consultants build their dream businesses?

I WROTE IT ALL IN A BOOK.

I have been writing this book for almost half a year and this is going to be the best written professional book of my life. However, I share a secret with you. In March, I threw half of the book to the trash bin. I felt that it was not good enough and did not give the extent of value that could stay in the book. By doing that, I made the whole thing a bit harder, because I had to write all day and wait for the readers.

I paid careful attention to do a GOOD job, I did not rush.

I would like to help other businesses to be built up by the help of the book.

He has loads of free time and he is constantly on a holiday.

Most entrepreneurs are in the office the whole day and work hard. He thinks he has to control everything, therefore he has very little free time and he rarely sees his family.

In contrast with that, digital millionaires work from home and they spend the whole day with their families. They withdraw and work remotely in silence if it is necessary therefore they are much more productive than those who go to work to the office.

If I was asked to tell what the best thing was about the lifestyle of an expert, I would say: freedom. You can be wherever you want to be, whenever you want to be and can unwind even for 1-2 months without having any problem from that.

The photo was taken in 2018 while on a 30 day holiday in Corfu ☺

We return to Corfu from time to time and spend 3-4 weeks in the camping of Paleokastritsa. We set up a tent and go on an excursion during the day or we bath. We reply the e-mails in the evening and work a few hours if it is needed. However, in most cases a maximum of 1 hour is enough to be done with the daily tasks. In winter, I work one or two days a week and the automated system does the sales. I love this kind of freedom because I can do what I feel like doing and

whenever I want to.

Think over what you want. Do you want a freer life that you fill with travel and experience? Then expert business is the key that you will need.

You can live a balanced and happy life.
Most entrepreneurs run in the treadwheel the whole day and spend only the weekend with the family. There are ones who work even then but that is not good as they become the slaves to their own businesses. There are periods when I work at the weekend as well but

it is becoming more and more seldom because I want to provide a happy life for my family.

A Digital Millionaire runs his business rather smartly and uses online tools that can automate all the customer care and profit making procedures.

Everybody aspires to live a balanced and happy life however, there are only few who can make it happen. When business goes well, many of them dig even deeper into it and lose connection with the rest of the world. They do not even realize when their children are already grown up…

I wish you a kind of life that makes it possible for you to be happy and spend more time with your family. You will feel the change of quality in your life even after the first month. You can be with your loved ones more and will not miss such important events like the first steps of your child.

I remember when in 2007 my first, elder daughter Lili was born. As an expert, I was working from home and was able to see her first steps and could hear her first words as well.

This has a priceless value to me. I am so glad that I did not only put a blanket on my children before they fell asleep, but they had grown up in front of my eyes.

In my opinion, this is the greatest advantage of knowledge based sales businesses besides providing a stable income.

He/She can afford anything, but does not outspend

You can train even thousands of people therefore your income is going to be higher. It is an indescribable feeling when you change and you do not sell your time anymore but your knowledge. You will remember the moment when while being on a holiday and you realize that you have earned money in your pay-box. I love when while skiing I get an order and earn money. ☺

In my book, I will call money many times a power resource, so please make this as an element of your own mindset. Money does not come to you to turn into a luxury car or expensive clothes. Money will love you if you manage it well.

The smarter you use this power source the more money will flow into your pocket. Your invested money will call the money in the pockets of other people and will persuade them to transfer it to your pocket.

Be aware as the basic purpose of your money is to flow. It would like to be transferred to the bank account of another person. You must pay attention to retain more money and to invest it, rather than spending it on unnecessary things.

GOAL: To retain and invest as much money as just possible.

Pay attention and be aware of these if you would like to deal with money smarter:

1.) I constantly look at how I can save money
I examine each and every time how I can save an amount of money by reconsidering shopping habits as well as the greater expenses I need to pay for. When I need any equipment for cutting my videos I check where I can buy it for the best price and I make my decision about the purchase accordingly. Then later I invest the saved amount in campaigns which generate further income.

2.) If we can, we stay in a tent not in a hotel
In the past 3 years we spent one month in Corfu in average. Considering our budget we could have spent one week only from the same amount of money if we had stayed in a 4 star hotel. We were freer in the camping and we also got more experience.

3.) We do not spend on status symbols
Believe me that I could afford buying the newest model of mobile phones for all my family members instead of the old one they have. But that $3.000 would be missing from the marketing budget. There are many people who license a luxury car because that is the way how they award themselves. An E class Mercedes starts from $ 80.000 and the insurance is also really expensive for this type of model. You can spend even $ 100.000 on a stuff you do not even need.

Money is going to be such a power source in your hand that you can use to reach incredible results. If you manage your money wisely, your business will constantly grow by your investments.

4.) A digital millionaire is exposed to minimal amount of stress, therefore lives longer than the average

What would you think if on the street someone stepped to you and offered you plus 5 years? What would you answer? Would you ask for it? YES? Then I have good news for you because this book can help you with that.

Stress is one of the most horrible mass murderers. It kills 120.000 people annually unobtrusively all over the world. There are many who live a stressful way of life and they reassure themselves with the illusion that it is normal as stress is an everyday phenomenon. Many entrepreneurs set goals which they are unable to achieve without stress.

I know what I am talking about. From 2006 to 2014 I pushed such a hard work into our business that we reached an annual $100.000 income. Many people would have been in my shoes but stress was in the background which tried to kill me slowly. In 2014 after a business negotiation in the morning I started feeling dizzy and my blood pressure went up.

Unfortunately, the doctor on duty mistreated me and I did not get the right treatment in time. By the evening I was taken to hospital and was given an MRI examination, where the doctor discovered 2 tiny dots which were the obvious sign of stroke. For two days they were not sure whether I would survive it or not but after 7 days I recovered and was sent back home. I started building my automated online business right after that moment which has been producing stable income since then till this day.

His best friends are his competitors (Yes, his concurrents!)
In real life entrepreneurs are hostile with their rivals and think that concurring companies steal customers.

The truth however is that there is ABUNDANCE in the world.

The other thing that I had to realize is that my best partners will come out from among my rivals.

The reason for this is that you target the same audience and you can generate much higher income by empowering each other. I know, it is hard to digest this information first, but I am certain that you will find positive emulants by who being united with you can achieve enormous breakthrough. Recently, I have been able to create more operating and greatly profitable affiliate partnerships. I am lucky because we constantly build a positive relationship and we mutually support each other.

We build a WIN-WIN situation by that I commend them and they also commend me. Due to this, we can reach even 250.000 customers with a single campaign.

The secret here are loyalty and trust. As long as you find good partners, getting new customers will not be a problem for long years. Your partners will commend you in e-mails and in social media posts, then you pay commission to them after those purchases which your partners brought in by their own direct codes.

How to use this book efficiently?

I would like to help you with using this book in a way that it should not be only another book on your bookshelf what you read and then just put aside. I really recommend you to highlight the important things while reading.

First of all, read and comprehend the topics of the book
If you encounter phrases you do not know, then search them in Google and find out their meanings. I wrote this book to be comprehensible to anyone but one or two jargons can occur.

I think that if you have a minimum knowledge about marketing or about how to start your enterprise, then this is not going to be a problem and you will be able to take the maximum out of my book.

Read it again and start using it in practice
This is a short and quickly readable book, therefore I ask you to read it first and then comprehend it. Then you read it again + make notes and complete the workbook.

You can start a successful millionaire business from this book of you read it many times and you process all the knowledge that I share with you. This is followed by realization, that many people are afraid of, but I encourage you to get started and if you need any help, you will find online courses on my website which are going to help you getting over the execution of the seemingly difficult steps.

Your business will not start by reading this book but if you are willing to invest the necessary time, money and energy, you will reach the goal that you set for yourself.

If I could build a successful online enterprise, with my help, you will be able to do it as well.

Who is Michael Tóth and why should you trust him?

Before we have a go with reading the book, I would like to introduce myself, because it is important for you to understand that if I could build this up, you will also be able to do the same.

I want to show my journey and the obstacles through which I built up my first online expert business. This path was not an easy one, but for you it is going to be much easier with my help.

I started my career as a marketing expert and a web developer.
The first internet company that hired me was Webreklám LTD. I learnt the fundamental knowledge of my profession there and faced many challenges that made me stronger.

I learnt programming and marketing in those years. Facebook and YouTube had not existed at that time yet, there were only content and affiliate marketing as tools for attracting customers.

My professional knowledge was improving fast due to the many customers I dealt with. Every day was a new challenge and due to that I had improved tremendously. Later the knowledge that I gained there, was the foundation of my first business that I build upon.

In 2004 I learnt a very exciting thing in Belgium.
The year 2004 was a turning point in my life as I was offered a job by a Belgian company. It was hard to break away from my Love and from my family but I felt that my life was changing radically. Actually, there I became independent and I was driving around Belgium by a company car while I was helping clients with online developments.

In 2005 we started our first own enterprise
The first year was very hard but we had been improving continuously and our team had been growing as well. More and more clients commissioned us with web development and the preparation of the related marketing campaigns. In 9 years we helped more than 1.000 businesses to get clients online.

In 2014 I had to change immediately because of the stroke
Due to the workload and the enormous amount of stress I had a stroke after which I really had to change. Online training seemed to be the best opportunity therefore I started a project. I trained thousands of entrepreneurs with my courses how to get clients online.

In 2019 the breakthrough came what I had been preparing myself for
An idea came up that an online conference should be organized where from in the morning till night, in 5 days, the best national experts would help national entrepreneurs. The Online Marketing Summit was born from this idea for which more than 16.000 entrepreneurs and company leaders signed up.

In around one and a half month I invested $20.000 in Facebook campaigns which made $30.000 income. Therefore, after the subtraction of the expenses $10.000 profit was realized by that new online conference. For the breakthrough a novelty was needed that had never existed before. It was a huge success, and this is what I can be thankful for everything in what I had achieved.

2020 The birth of the Book
I was curious about whether there was a need for the knowledge I had obtained in years. I asked 100 of my followers whether they found the idea of online business attractive that provides stress free, stable income.

The market research I did gave a definite "YES" as an answer.

After that the sequence of events speeded up as I started writing my book and worked out my whole product-value pyramid. Yes, I make online courses beside the book so as not only to hold out a carrot with others but also to help them realize their knowledge based online business work.

Until 2030 I am going to help 10.000 entrepreneurs to start their businesses. I have a dream… I will show this opportunity to 100.000 readers of mine and with 10.000 from among them we are also going to build up a business of that kind.

With this mission of mine I can help broadly 25.000 or 30.000 people in 10.000 families. It means that 10.000 families can live a more relaxed, happier life in a way that they reach above an average income monthly. I am lucky to be able to change so many people's lives by this book and the online courses build on it.

As you can see I am not motivated by money. We need the amount of money that provides us a comfortable standard of life. We can call this an early retirement as well, as in fact, we do not have to work so hard in knowledge based enterprises.

Can someone as well become a Digital Millionaire who is not an expert in any field?

I would like to make it clear for you in the beginning that you do not need any qualification for a business of this kind. The truth is that no one will ever require a certificate from you, but they will expect you to share the knowledge you obtained and that way improve your customers.

Maybe you think that this is not for you as you do not have anything that you are better at than the average. This is a false way of thinking as people acquire enormous amount of knowledge in long years that can be a priceless value to others...

- You make enticing meals and bake sweet miracles?
- Your hobby is playing the guitar and you are also good at it?
- You speak a language on a professional level?
- Your meaning of life is fitness and eating clean?
- Your friends always talk to you whenever they have problems?
- Everyone is looking for you with one particular thing?

Yes? Then congratulations, because you have a greater knowledge than the average and there are thousands of people out there who desire this knowledge.

By this book I will bring the maximum out of you.

Now get rid of all the pessimistic and negative thoughts which were engraved in your mind. Fall off the tree, go and fall off your bicycle or do anything else that your parents brought you up against.

You have to get all the false programming codes out of your head that was implanted in you by others and we are going to exchange them for good thoughts.

It is not the degree that makes and expert but the greatest value that is knowledge

The greatest mistake in life, if in the future, you rely on what you learnt in traditional education. Unfortunately, schools 15-20 years are lagging behind recent technology. Therefore we must not trust traditional education exclusively or rely on it. It is a good example if we compare and freshly graduated student in marketing to an entrepreneur who accomplished 3-4 courses, gained experience and read books. This entrepreneur will make more efficient campaigns than the freshly graduated youngster.

KNOWLEDGE and gained EXPERIENCE are the VALUES that you must share with other people and you must share them in a way that enables you to make a living on it.

Tony Robbins, the best paid life coach

Tony had already helped many with solving problems in a way that he had not acquired any certification for it. I know it is weird as in many people's eyes he is a person who worth attention and the best thoughts come from. The question is that if Tony could achieve to be loved by millions and become the world No.1 Life Coach without certificates, then why are you still thinking about diplomas? Tony Robbins built his company without degrees, relying exclusively on his own experience and wisdom.

Value is more important than certificates. The greater values you give your clients, the greater amount of success you will achieve.

Steve Jobs left university and what happened was...

The truth is that Steve Jobs left school because he was not engrossed by it and he had different plans. I do not encourage you to leave school but to understand that certificate is insufficient.

Steve started working seriously on realizing his ideas after leaving school and the products that completely transformed our times had been born from these ideas.

He revolutionized mobile phones and he provided new gadgets like iPad and Mac operational system. All of these would have been inaccessible if he had not had experience and knowledge.

Your knowledge and your experience worth 1.000 times more than any degree
The 2 previous examples I think comforted you that not only trained teacher with diplomas can make knowledge based online enterprises. You must look for the knowledge in yourself that thousands desire and you have got to share it with them.

How can you become a Knowledge Commerce Millionaire?
Anyone can be a successful online entrepreneur but you have to learn the basics. This book will help you with that and if you understand how it works, you can build it up in simple steps.
The title of the book maybe suggests that this is a millionaire training and it is enough to think about it, but I disprove that. An enormous

amount of work is ahead you and you will have to improve yourself continuously.

You can bring the best out of your own self if you continuously improve yourself.

1.) How to become a

well-paid expert?

1.) HOW TO BECOME A WELL-PAID EXPERT

The market rewards your work in a way that the money from the bank account of your customers will be transferred to your bank account. Basically, money loves travelling and meet new people.

The challenge here is not to earn a lot of money but to retain and invest as much as you can. By investing money you will reach a greater mass of people and that way your income will grow as well as the number of your customers day by day.

The right financial mindset is outstandingly important in expert businesses. You cannot afford buying a Ferrari or a luxury home after your first great success. You must be smarter than the average entrepreneurs and that way you can reach greater results.

It does not matter if you are not a trained graduate expert
I had already written about that in the previous chapter but now I would like to dig deeper into it with you as this is the No.1 excuse why many do not start it at all.

IT IS IMPORTANT. No one will require a degree from you.
I would like to comfort you that none of your customers will require you to present your degree. It is simple and logical that if they are given value then a part of them will buy from you. I have never heard from any expert that the customer asked for a degree before making a decision. Degrees are necessary for those who would like a stable life as an employee but this does not exist anymore.

Build on your strength, in what you are a champion
You have to find the thing that you are smarter at than the average and you will have to build upon that. Many of my clients had already said: "Mike, I am average in everything. What should I do?" It is really interesting that in most cases within 1 hour of coaching we find that only one thing.

You are also a world champion in something but it is not enough because if nobody is interested in this strength of yours, it will be unmarketable. I have many clients who are world champion in one or two everyday activities. There are some of them who know the complete Italian cuisine, but you can also find some who had been playing the drums for 25 years. When you reach the level of mastery there will not be a bell ringing to warn you "Hey, you have become a world champion." and you will not be given a trophy either, but these are the things that millions crave for.

There are many who covet to be able to make a pizza like what is made in the best Italian restaurants. Do you know the recipe and the steps of preparation? Share it with them and start an Italian online cooking course where thousands will learn cooking techniques from you that is going to make their lives happy.

It is not a question that you are going to be a world champion but what if indeed you are not outstandingly strong at anything?

What should I do if I am not outstanding in anything?
Ok, calm down, it does not matter. Remember, when you were a child you could not ride the bicycle either. How many times did you have to fall by the time you were able to careen? You have to take that journey now. You have to learn and study from books, from courses and you have to choose mentors, who are the experts of that certain field.

In 10.000 hours you can master anything.
I would not like to scare you but you need a lot of self-development. Maybe 10.000 hours is extreme and 5.000-6.000 hours of learning and experience will be enough for you.

The reason why I am writing about 10.000 hours is because there are serious topics for what you need minimum that amount of time. Certainly, there are fields where you can find yourself among the bests within a couple of thousands of hours, but undoubtedly, you will have to improve yourself continuously in the future.

You have to count on that you will need to read minimum 4-5 books and make notes as well as process them to integrate them in your knowledge. Besides that you will also have to accomplish online courses and watch YouTube videos in that topic. Let's add the thousands of blog posts to all of these which help deepen your knowledge. It will not be easy but the good news is that your business can already be started in the beginning of your self-development.

There is no need to possess the knowledge of a university professor to make millions of an income
Find the knowledge you have above the average and share it in YouTube videos, in blog posts and on your Facebook + Instagram accounts. Do not be afraid if you are not a professor. Just help others. The more valuable knowledge you share the more followers you will have hence you will end up with more potential customers. You can start easily and create the foundation of you online enterprise by using free tools.

Self-development + Practice = VALUABLE KNOWLEDGE

There are many people who are fanatic self-developers but they do not use the knowledge and do not gain any experience. There are those who obtain a great amount of experience in a way that they do not develop themselves.

My personal experience with my clients is that outstanding results can be achieved if both are present. You can only give value if these are together in your hands.

Learning is one of the best things you can do even if you dislike traditional school training. My good news is that you can be the one who decide what you learn, when you learn it and from who. You have to make the right decision to keep the right direction and hence you acquire valuable knowledge which you can sell later.

As an expert you need to improve yourself continuously
Unfortunately, it is not enough for you to be good at something now, because if you do not improve, you will fall behind. There are professions where things change on a daily basis and therefore it is especially important to have an up-to-date expertise in those fields. Marketing is a great example for this, which changes daily. More and more recent tactics and tools are coming out that you have to know and try in order to be able to give the most to your followers and to your customers.

Did you know that each and every book you read changes you a bit? Each and every video or online course adds a little to the knowledge you already have. As for me, I improve my knowledge especially in the field of marketing and I enjoy when I learn new things.

Apply what you had already learnt and gain experience
After reading a book apply what you have learnt and gain experience. This is the way how a book turns into valuable knowledge. The same thing I observed with online courses. When I just watched the courses but did not apply the knowledge I obtained, I was not able to pass it on to my customers. However, when I applied the acquired knowledge step by step, I could share it with others.

Abraham Lincoln said that:

"Give me 6 hours for cutting down a tree, and in the first four, I shall spend with sharpening the axe."

How much time are you going to spend with sharpening your axe before you get started? Each and every minute you spend with self-improvement and applying the knowledge, it will sharpen your axe and the sharper it is going to be, the easier it will be for you to cut down the tree.

Share valuable knowledge and experience with others
There are many who procure knowledge but they do not share it with others. As for an expert, it will be your duty to hand on the knowledge you obtained to others. This is the basis of your Knowledge Commerce enterprise. Imagine what would happen if everyone kept his or her knowledge for themselves. Everything would simple stuck and nothing would improve in life.

Sharing is caring. Sharing = Caring. I would like to encourage you to pass on all the knowledge you have to those who are willing to pay for it.

What makes your knowledge valuable to others?
They pay for it and then they can use it to transform their lives with it. Certainly, a lead magnet and lots of free contents are needed, but if you would like to get result with your customers, they must pay for your knowledge and experience.

There are plenty of examples which prove that if someone does not pay for a particular knowledge, there is no inspiring power for him or for her to use it as well. The internet is full of free, available information but most of them will not transform your life in reality.

Let's have a look at an example that shows what makes your knowledge valuable that you offer to your customers:

Lead magnet material: FREE
Its main purpose is to make you known to your target audience and build trust in them. Later you can get better results when you sell your irresistible offer due to your lead magnet.

Admission product: $7-$37
It has only one function which is to segment customers from those who are only interested in free material. It is to make the first purchase happen and cut the costs of advertisement.

Core product: $997-$3.997
This is a more painful decision for the customer because the price is higher and therefore the level of dedication as well.

He or she has to spend more time with your course and pay a higher amount of money. Here it can be observed that whoever purchases your offer, he or she wants to make progress and get results.

Profit maximizing: $2.997-$49.970
This is your high ticket offer that only few will pay due to its high price. The lucky ones who buy this offer from you will work much harder. You will also have an easier job than with those customers who get this one for free. I saw it with many clients that those who got a more expensive learning material for free, they simply would not do it. They did not pay for it so therefore there is no real inspiration why they would push it hard. Just think it over, if you spent $9-997 on a coaching program, how seriously you would take it? The answer is: VERY MUCH.

Everyone feels therefore it is important that if you offer your knowledge for free or below price, it simply will not be taken seriously.

How can you valorize the knowledge within you?
It is a really good question and we need to talk about many things before you put a price tag on your knowledge. You have to decide whether you sell to masses on a low price or your knowledge will be accessible exclusively for a high price. Certainly, it can be the combination of both, when your entrance product reaches thousands on a surprisingly low price and the second step is an already high priced offer. Do not underestimate your knowledge, because what is in your mind worth gold for many.

How can you reach a $15.000 of income according to the example?
    1.) 200 of your customers buy your entrance product for $7
    2.) 10 of your customers buy your core product for $997

3.) 1 customer buy your profit maximizing product for $3.497

In the previous page the third offer was a high ticket offer that only few will take. I do not understand because it is much easier to sell to 2 customers than to convince 200.

Get more than possible potential customers from point A to point B
Every problem is similar as your customer would like to get from the current not too ideal condition to the desired one. We can demonstrate this by getting the customer from point A to point B.

This is going to be the customer's route which will show by what steps he or she can move forward with your help.

Example: You play the guitar really well and you would like to make a living with that. Your task is to write down the whole route which gets your customer to the professional level of playing the guitar.

This journey will have steep hills and obstacles but with your help anyone can reach the top of the mountain. You will be the person who has already climbed the mountain therefore many people will trust you. This kind of trust will strengthen your sales and self-brand.

Build positive and fruitful relationships

The greatest effect multiplier of the expert businesses are the quality relationships and lists. You have to build positive and value based relationships with your competitors, as there will be many of them who is going to become your affiliate partners in the future. The other powerful tool is the self-owned list. This can be an e-mail list or the overall number of followers in the site if a social media group. The better the quality of your potential customer list is the higher income you can realize in the future.

How can you build a quality list?

1.) Relevant lead magnet and content: You have to build your free materials and contents specifically related to the problems of your target audience. That way the ratio of the read e-mails you send will be much greater.

2.) Continuous communication: Do not confuse this one with sales because if sales happen more often than value share your e-mail list will burn out really fast and you will end up with a low income. The other mistake is that if you rarely communicate, you will be forgotten and it will increase the number of people who unsubscribe from your newsletters.

3.) Proper targeting: You have to target very precisely with your advertisement campaigns in order to reach your target audience. Unfortunately, if your ad appears to the irrelevant people, it is going to be expensive for you to advertize and later your offer will not be taken the way it should be. This has a very simple reason… They are

NOT interested in your offer as they do not have a problem that your product or service can solve.

Your greatest effect multiplier is going to be building relationships

You have to be known by an increasing number of masses in order to reach the sufficient amount of buyers. You can build relationships in two different ways: online and offline.

Building relationship online is simple because you go to an offline networking event and you can meet at least 100 new potential customers. If your buyers are not entrepreneurs, but ordinary people, you can also find events or group meetings that your buyers attend regularly.

Building relationships online is also simple, but it can be quicker if you put your online system together smartly. This can be a simple lead magnet that can be downloaded as an exchange for providing their e-mail addresses. The other solution is when you offer a free consultation where you can help the potential buyers so that way you make them engaged.

Build fruitful relationships with your potential buyers

A relationship will be fruitful if you share value in advance and do not expect anything in return immediately. We use gratitude as a psychological press button when we would like to sell a high priced offer.

Another well functioning solution when you build relationships in a mass in a way that you continuously send valuable contents to the people who are interested in your product or service. This also works just perfectly and you can increase the level of trust in masses. The best is if you send videos or share them on YouTube.

Look for affiliate partners among your competitors
I know it is quite bold for the first time because the majority of entrepreneurs think that a competitor is an enemy. I would like to get this out of your head by presenting a few examples:

1.) One or two affiliate partners of mine pays me $10.000 commission in average as an exchange for the affiliations I provide them.
2.) I have good relationship with most of my competitors, which is proved most by the fact that I could organize the Online Marketing Summit conference 3 times subsequently, where I made interviews with my fellow rivals.
3.) I feel many times that they are my friends and I can turn to them for help if I have any problems.

As you can see this is a new opportunity you have to live with. Avoid those concurrences who harmed you in any way and build relationship with those who are sincere, positive and believe that together you are able to achieve more.

Building an own community on Facebook
I left this for the end, it is the best though. Build a private Facebook group where there are your customers and build also another one separately where there are those who subscribe to your lead magnet. In both groups communicate and share value continuously. An own community (tribe) can be a huge opportunity in your marketing. They support you, protect you and help you if fate brings it forward.

Ask them what their problem is and offer a solution

We came to an important stage as we need to find out what kind of problems your customers are struggling with. You can ascertain this by market research and you will know from the answers what they need your help with. You can even make titles of online lecture courses from the words that can be found in the answers. More people will buy from you if you use the words and expressions of your buyers in your courses.

The successful expert asks questions continuously and collects materials

I recommend you to do market research before you plan your online course and ask your customers what the biggest problems are they struggle with.

You will have plenty of opportunities beyond the market research to collect data. One of these tools is bucket.io by which you can collect information on your opt-in subscribing pages. This excellent tool transforms the process of subscription and asks a few questions that can be answered by a simple click.

You can also use Facebook for data collection where you can receive a lot of interesting information from a vote or from answers given by asking simple question. The same works really well on Instagram as well. You can use tools in your story there, you can ask or people can vote.

Certainly, apart from these opportunities you have loads of options where you can collect useful information. You do not have to insist exclusively on online platforms, you can gather data on offline events or on conferences as an exhibitor.

Simply market research campaign by Google sheets
Google sheets provide the simplest solution to do a quick, market research questionnaire. You can use it for free and make the questionnaire within minutes.

Consider the fact that people do not like long and time consuming sheets therefore only few of them fill them in. Be careful with asking questions, ask the ones only you really need. Do not extend the size of the questionnaire with unnecessary questions as it is not going to not help you either with the planning of your online course.

In the past few years I did several market research questionnaires that helped me with making my courses. In these ones I asked 3 questions and I got to know the problems and real needs of my potential customers.

1.) What is your biggest problem that makes you stay awake at night? What is the one thing that you think about every day?

2.) What would you ask from me if there were only the two of us sitting in front of each other and you could ask only one question?

3.) What do you think, how could I help you to solve this problem?

It is enough to ask these 3 questions and you will get answers that you can use immediately. You can use a part of these in your marketing texts, campaigns, but also in your online courses as the different modules or titles of your lectures.

How should you make valuable learning material from the answers of a questionnaire?
The answers you get are really valuable as they are written in the language of your customers and they describe the same problem. The words and sentences you are given work really well as the titles of your online lectures as well.

Here is an example for an answer which I used as the title of a video course that I made:

"How can I make an original Italian pizza like the one that is made by Italian chefs in Italy?"

We take the important elements out of this question and we create a title that will raise attention. The most important here are the desire and the result that they would like to reach. The title of the course lecture that you create from the question therefore would be the following:

„This is how you make original Italian pizza in a few simple steps."

Your potential buyers will be curious immediately about the recipe that enables them to make a real, Italian pizza. You can make a sentence that catches your buyers' attention and feels that this course is for them.

Use the answers in your marketing material

Use the incoming answers in your marketing material as well. It is probable that if 20 of the questioned potential buyers use the same words from 100 – if you apply these in ads – then more of them will respond to your advertisement. Write every marketing text as if your customer said it and the success of your campaign will be guaranteed.

Consider money as a power resource and invest it.

I would like to make you consider money as a power resource by this book. Many make a mistake and start dispend money but that is a wrong decision. Instead of outspending, choose investment and you will be able to grow faster. This is a special power source that can multiply the number of people who are interested in your product.

Let me represent this with an example:

1,)You earn $3.000 and you spend the money on luxury products. In that case your money will not produce any more profit but you will have some new stuff that will get dusted at home.

2.)You earn $3.000 and you invest the whole amount in online advertizing. From this amount of money you can reach approximately 1.000 new potential customers. There will be around 500 from among them who will ask for your lead magnet and there will be 50 who will buy from you as well. In the worst case you will have 30 new buyers who are going to spend $30-$100 on your products or services.

In each and every case investment is a better decision than dispending. Even if you decide to move more carefully and you invest only 10-20% in advertizing you can multiply your income within one year in that case as well. Think about what an enormous amount of growth you can reach with one single smart decision.

Money will help to make you known to more and more people
Your money as a power resource is a visibility vest as the greater amount you can invest in your Knowledge Commerce business the faster you can move forward.

You do not have to be concerned about money because you can build it up slowly and carefully. It is not even a problem either if you can start with only a small amount of an investment but reinvest in your own enterprise as much as you can.

Be your own financial investor.

As the first step examine how much of a risk it is to invest in this business. How marketable is your idea? If you feel that success is stable and predictable, invest the greatest amount you just can in the beginning and reinvest continuously from your taxed profit.

MENTOR: Choose a mentor and speed up
This book and my courses will help you to reach a certain point but you will feel when you have to step on to the next level. Then you will need a mentor who has already accomplished the route which is ahead of you in the coming years.

Look around what kind of mentors can help you and buy books or online courses from them. After that, examine how you can work with them later. A mentor can reduce the time even by years which you need for the breakthrough. You can work together with more mentors but it works only if you have enough time for everything. You must learn and apply the knowledge of your mentor. Most of the entrepreneurs cannot reach the big breakthrough because they do not have a mentor or they do not spend enough time with realization.

A good mentor shows the direction and gives the tools in your hands that you will need.

Invest your money in your knowledge instead of luxury products
A new iPhone, a laptop or even a luxury car can be very tempting. This temptation will be there each and every single day whenever a successful campaign brings millions of income.

If you cannot resist the temptation, you are a consumer. If you invest in your knowledge, you are a Knowledge Millionaire.

The fact that if you watch YouTube videos all they, you are a consumer can also be connected to this. If you produce YouTube video contents, you are a content creator. The less you should consume contents and the more you should create contents. It is interesting that there are millionaires who are on Facebook but their profiles have not been updated for several years. These entrepreneurs know it really well that making contents will bring money and consumption is going to take it away.

Each and every wasted hour on YouTube or on Facebook means a severe loss of income for you. Imagine if in 2 hours you do not watch videos but make 2 own videos which thousands of people will watch after.

Each and every dollar invested in building contact lists pays off
I have been saying to my clients to build lists for years now. Many think that this is unnecessary because they do not understand how lists work. They are afraid of unsubscriptions, therefore they do not even initiate measurable campaigns. The amount that you invest in building lists pays off if you follow the right strategy.

Did you know that each and every subscriber produces a $4 income? Let's assume that you build a quality list by a smart lead magnet and you spend $1.000 on the whole. This is going to bring around 200 subscribers therefore every e-mail of yours will be read by 60-80 people. From among this amount of interested buyers there will be 8 or 10 who is going to make purchase so 1 e-mail can make you even $500.

Imagine how incredible results you could reach by a list of 10.000 if you send 5-6 emails in a campaign.

Number of subscribers who receive your e-mails: 10.000 persons
Number of subscribers who open your e-mails: 1.500-2.000 persons
Number of readers who clink on the link: 150-200 persons
Number of visitors who buy immediately: 10-15 persons

If your offer worth $100, by sending 1 e-mail, you can reach around $1.000 income. However, if you send 3 e-mails in every 2-3 days and another 2 e-mails on the closing day of the campaign (1 in the morning and 1 in the evening) you will end up with sending 5 e-mails in total. Therefore the 5 e-mails can bring you even above $3.000. Certainly, if the price is higher the income can increase but the number of buyers can fall as well.

Invest in campaigns instead of gambling
I have never been a big gambler. I simply cannot rely on making my own income dependent from another person despite of the fact that many people do that even if the chance of winning is minimal. Actually, I would like to convince you not to spend on this at all.

Acquire the investor and donator mindset
Knowledge Commerce carries great opportunities for you but 2 mindsets are necessary for them. Both of them are essential and related to money management.

1.)The investor mindset:
An investor uses all his or her money to increase the income in his or her bank account. He or she invests his or her money consciously and if there is something that is loss making, he or she quits from it.

2.)The donator mindset:
The donator pays attention to give back to the community and supports issues that he or she can identify with. He or she feels joy if he or she supports people for whom the donated amount means a greater value.

Applying these two mindsets together will make you a better person and will influence your thoughts. On a subconscious level you combine the profit making idea and the opportunity of donation. Many people donate because they feel guilty of earning a lot of money. A good example for this is when a donator throws some coins to the hat of a homeless while walking on the way back home. This is a good deed and it makes you a better person.

I think you should never feel guilty if you earn a lot of money. If someone puts a huge amount of work into his or her dream project he or she can also reach his or her goal. For this however you will need the two mindsets above and you need to live accordingly. I noticed that for me giving is a better feeling than receiving. Donate bravely and happily.

Dare to dream. Thousands of customers are waiting for you

You must forget doubt and if you close your eyes you have to see yourself as you better the lives of thousands as a recognized expert. Visualization is one of the best tools to engrave your goals in your subconscious mind. It is not enough to write down your goals on a daily basis.

Practice: Close your eyes and imagine where you are going to be in 5-10 years. Who are the ones surrounding you? Where do you live? What kind of life do you have? How much do you work? How many people do you help? What kind of results do you achieve? How does it feel to be successful?

The practice above will help you to tackle doubt hiding within you and you will be able to think big.

Do not settle for small successes. Aim for the top.
When I ask you how much money you want to earn, I ask you to think of as a high amount as possible. When you set a goal too low, you will put less energy to the work. The lower the target is the easier you can reach the goal you set. Imagine that you owe someone $ 3.000 and you have to pay the debt back in a couple of weeks. What would you do if time urged you? Would you leave no stone unturned? Would you call your former customers? Would you try new tools?

The majority of people – if necessary – are able to be superhuman. I remember when the tax authorities notified me that there were mistakes in my bookkeeping. Suddenly, it cost $15.000 to fix it, and the amount was not available for me at that moment. What did I do? First, I felt under the weather and lost enthusiasm in everything.

After that I started thinking how I could take possession of this amount as quickly as possible. I worked out a complex coaching program and then I found 12 buyers in one week. These 12 clients paid me more than $15.000 for a 3 months program.

You can reach even $120.000 income annually
There are many who settle for $1.000 monthly, but there are some others who set the $10.000 monthly goal as an income. The greater the goal is the harder you work on reaching it.

As they reach $10.000 income monthly they start planning immediately, how they could reach $20.000. This is the way they are moving forward and they do not even notice when they approach $50.000 income monthly which means $600.000 annually.

You may think that this is just a dream but anyone can make it happen. Employees optimize their expenses on their monthly salary therefore they give up on their dreams. They have no striving after development within them and this is how they live their whole lives. As a contrast, development and growth are the most important for entrepreneurs.

As an entrepreneur it is your obligation to earn as much money as possible so to help thousands of customers and beside that to build a team. A well-functioning Knowledge Commerce enterprise can provide stable monthly income to at least 20-30 families. In the beginning you will be alone and make slow progress but the greater challenges you face the more colleagues you will need to hire.

2.) Let's Plan

Your Expert Business

2.) Let's plan your Expert Business

I believe that now you understand how great the opportunity is in front of you and I will help you in this second chapter to plan your online business based on your knowledge. We will examine why it is worth for you to start and what you have to be careful with while building your own business.

First of all, I would like to ask you to delete negative thoughts that are associated with the word "GURU". For a while, there are many people who build negative thoughts enthusiastically that can be easily attached to people and will remain with them for the rest of their lives… therefore they are unsuccessful.

There will be many who says to you that *"Why do you get down to it? There are enough experts already…"* or *"Every second entrepreneur now is a consultant…"* All of these will come from sober people who are bitter and they had already given up. They will live their whole lives in that form and everyone else will be blamed because of their fate.

This is going to change when you will have helped thousands. When this is noticed, a part of the critics will say: *"I told you. I knew you were going to make it."* Try to process it and note that do not start negative campaigns and do not be negative at all. Smile and be enduring and someone who makes things happen. You will be the one who knows exactly what you have to build up and how much time it takes to reach the goal you set for yourself.

As an expert you have to invest a greater amount of work in the beginning and you have to improve faster than the others. What do you think how did I become an expert? Did it just happen?

Well, the answer is NO. In 2014 I had double stroke and then I started building myself and my self-brand as a consultant. In the first years I did not earn much but I enjoyed it because the books and the American training courses lifted me up to unimaginable heights.

Yes, I am talking about my knowledge. I did not earn much but in theory I reached the level of the great mentors.

This was what was missing and I felt it in each and every moment…

Experience is the most important component of knowledge.

The 6 greatest advantages of an expert business

Are you ready to let me take your whole life upside down? Are you ready for allowing me to delete everything from your life that is „normal" and set up a completely new system? Expert business is good and bad as well, but I am going to explain this in details in the following 9 points.

1. Do what you love and teach it to others as well.

I ask you to have a go with it if you have a hobby or an activity that you love. If you find it, from then on, you are not going to work anymore but you live for your hobby.

Let's say that you are working for a bank currently and you feel that this job is killing you, you cannot wait to finish it but you love playing the guitar. Whenever you have free time you play the guitar and you improve yourself. It can even happen that you play the hardest rock ballad while keeping your eyes closed. ☺

Well, if you feel that, you have to be an instructor of guitar playing. Ok, but how? I am not a music teacher. ☺

The good news is that in most cases you will not need and official certification because your buyers will not be interested in your diploma. Your buyers would like to know how to play the guitar in a way that you do therefore they are willing to learn from you for months.

You will notice that your buyers are going to be your best friends with whom you share your experience with joy. You are going to train and improve them with great enthusiasm for what they are happily invest their money in your knowledge.

This is where the road splits into two as there are people who do it for the money but the really successful Knowledge Commerce entrepreneurs teach because they are in love with that particular topic. Those who do it only for the money will vanish from the market within a few months. Therefore they will not be able to rise to the expert level. But those who pour their souls and hearts into it, because they love what they do, will reach much bigger success.

Sometimes I wish that there were not be 11 am already because I could still finish 2-3 e-mails or 1 sales landing. My devotion is tremendous and I am well aware that I am going to change the lives of ten thousands by my book as well as by my related trainings. I would like to leave something behind and I believe that it is already SOMETHING if I help thousands of people build a freer and richer life.

2. Build valuable relationships and create something new.

There are huge opportunities standing in front of you. One of the best alternatives to build relationships is when you build your own "tribe"who are happy to learn from you. You never know who of your contacts will bring you a huge outbreak therefore you have to pay attention to each and every one of your followers.

I can see that one or two (buyers) stands out from the crowd who becomes a fan of you and will recommend you. These people are your ambassadors, who are able to influence masses, therefore will bring you thousands of customers without you paying a dime for it.

Create something new. An innovation that your followers desire. Building relationships and the community of followers are really valuable because you can find out what problems they struggle with by a well-targeted market research. You can work out products which can be solutions to their problems. The key to success is the community that you build up and who are going to buy your knowledge e.g. in the form of an online course. The members of this community will be who provide you a stable income.

3. You can work from anywhere, anytime (Laptop style)
Yes, you can finally make it happen that you will not sit in an office the whole day. You do not have to commute every day but you can work from home. You can work comfortably, freely and according to your own schedule.

It is also possible that you move dream countries in every couple of months where others spend only a week vacation. I will teach you in this book how to use a system that you can build a business with and what is independent from place. I encourage you to live in countries that motivate you. You can make all your dreams come true if you build an online business and you can work at any time, from anywhere in the following years.

4. You will be free and you can work with whoever you just want to
Forget about bad clients. Many coaches suffer from the lack of clients therefore they work also with people who are only a pain in their neck. This must be changed. You are a free consultant who can decide who you would like to work with. You say no to energy vampires who are bothering you day and night and do not let you live your life. You say no to the negative, pessimistic and doubtful clients, who are continuously looking for your faults. You will not need any more headache and stress, because you are going to work with the bests. You will have clients who cooperate with you utterly and do what you ask from them. You can reach transformation and success only with these types of clients. The quality client does not tease and neither he or she makes a problem of anything.

You will recognize the bad type of client from a certain distance if you had already worked with some of them. One of the features is when he or she shares his or her doubts and bad experiences with you on the very first meeting. I have had many of this type of customer. ☹

I had a super negative client who started our first meeting like this:

"I hope that you are not going to fool me because the previous 3 programming companies deceived and stripped me really badly..."

Unfortunately, back then I was motivated by MONEY and I took this client as well saying that we would do the job honestly. The problem started with him expecting tasks from us which were not included in our contract with him. I went along with the game and we solved a couple of things for free but we had been continuously given extra tasks. When I said 'no' to him on the free job, suddenly we became the bad guys. ☹

5. Your success depends on your marketing and your value

Your marketing can be superb if you do not give real value. You need to balance these two things and you have to provide a kind of service that overfulfils the expectation of your clients.

Your clients expect 100% from you but if you do a bit more you will be THE BEST in their eyes. You will be given such a trust that means almost absolute attention. In many cases, one or two extra that they do not count on are enough and you give them such an experience with that which will be associated with your name in their minds.

You have to make sure that what you offer is valuable. It is worth testing and following the feedbacks. A part of the American consultants initiate a BETA test as the first step. They send the online course in a newsletter and give it away to 100 customers for a symbolic price. As an exchange they request a continuous feedback and the participants share every thought with the expert. They fine-tune the course by using the information they got from the customers that way.

6. The amount of money you earn equals with the amount of value you give

It does matter whether the value you share is average or priceless. Imagine a client who would like to play the guitar but is not brave enough to have a go at it. You make a general online course with the basics that helps acquire the skill of playing the guitar. This is the required basic that you have to offer but you can add extras to it that teach new, special techniques as well. This will increase value in such a way that means an immeasurable value category in the mind of your customer. I cannot emphasize it enough that you should overfulfil the expectations of your customers.

The amount that you can require for your online course will be dependent on the represented value you offer. It is worth increasing the value so to be able to request a higher price for the course.

How can you increase the represented and the real value? It is a good question but the examples show that you have to offer more elements than the experts who offer similar products or services like you. An offer is needed which is hard to refuse and you will have to have bonuses and extras for that.

What can be a good bonus? Further and short online courses, live lectures or webinars, downloadable books or checklists.

You have to be creative and you need to raise the represented value to the sky so that you can give a huge discount after that. Certainly, DO NOT sell your course for too much.

Let's say that you would like to sell your new online course for $997.

There are many experts who sell it immediately and offer their courses for half a price but this is not a good decision. Instead of doing that, pack your offer with a lot of bonuses and give a seemingly incredible discount from the represented price of your product. Adding the price of the bonuses e.g. a $9.997 will come out that you can offer a 90% bonus from and that way you can sell your online course for the real $997 price.

Value is the most important and if you are smart enough you will raise the represented value to such a level by the bonuses that most customers will take notice of it immediately. The higher the represented value is the greater the amount of discount you can give and you can sell on a higher price.

10 steps expert business building formula

I made a 10 steps process. If you follow it, by the end you will have the plan in your hand by which you will reach huge success. This formula will help you to build up your 6 figure business.

1. Choose your topic and become the master of it.

What is the thing that you do on a prominent level? What is that one thing you know better than others? Find what interests you the most. Most people spend more time with what makes them exhilarated. This is how talents are born. Those people who invest 10.000 hours into something that others who do only the portion of it. The more time you spend with an activity, the closer you will get to the expert level.

You do not even have to be concerned if you do not have an outstanding knowledge yet because if you choose a direction and invest 10.000 hours of learning and practice, you will reach the expert level. You can become the master of any field. It depends exclusively on you and your level endurance. It can also happen that you acquire this particular knowledge in a shorter period of time and you become a master by adding the relevant amount of practice.

DO NOT choose a field of expertise on the basis of the estimated income you can get out of it. There are many who train themselves to become an expert in a profession because they see huge amount of incomes but after a while they lose enthusiasm and then it becomes only a pain on their neck for them.

You can make a good decision if you feel each and every moment you spend with the chosen profession as a hobby not as work.

2. Choose your target audience (Niche market)

After choosing your field of special knowledge that makes you thrilled and what you would like to deal with joyfully in the following years, you have to start elaborating on your target audience.

It is important to plan your Avatar as precisely as you can in another word the profile of your dream customer. Write down the most data you can, so later it will serve you as a basis for positioning.

If you do not have any customers yet who could be asked, find as many people as you can who struggle with the same problem. Ask them and summarize the answers to the later data analysis. The received answers can later be used for product development, content marketing or in your advertizing campaigns.

What should you ask while doing market research? EVERYTHING.

Should I give it a name? YES. This will help you to form it as a character and later it is going to be easier to recall the features.

3. Find the critical problems of your target audience.

Successful online businesses start with market research and they develop their products on the basis of the results they get. In order to be able to do this you have to know what the critical problem is what makes them stay awake at night and what they would like to solve urgently.

How can you find this problem? ASK. Make a simple Google form with simple questions and send it to your e-mail list. You do not have an e-mail list? Then advertize the form.
Your market research list of queries can be longer but shorter as well. You have to test the amount of questions they are willing to answer. Encourage them with gifts so that more and more of them will share their problems with you. The more answers you receive, the clearer view you will have about their most regular problems.

You can also use these answers later in your online courses. I saw more American online courses that highlighted phrases/sentences from a market research and these became later the title of an online course. This is a super idea because your buyers feel that you speak their language and they feel that your course is for them. You can reach a higher conversion by using this simple technique.

4. **Write your story of how you became an expert (what positions you).**

You will be an authentic expert if you write your story. Storytelling is not easy but if you are smart enough, your story is going to be the most important element of your whole system.

While writing your story, feel free to think of movies. There is a hero and there are the obstacles which he or she has to tackle. These external and internal obstacles that you combat made you reach the point where you are standing right now. You had a critical problem that you solved successfully. You have to represent this transformation by using the right words. We know many successful stories. They all have one thing in common. They make us think and influence our emotions.

You have to apply the great story everywhere, because it strengthens your business and increase your results.

5. Work out the best solution to the problem.
Before you make any online courses, work out the fully comprehensive solution that solved the given problem. Your customers are looking for a solution which takes them from point A to point B. On this way, you are going to be their guide.

Example: Many people suffer from lower back pain and back pain. A lot of them try every medicine or cream but in most of the cases these are not effective enough.

Solution: If this is your field of expertise, work out an exercise program which helps relieve the pain or get rid of it completely. Make a video recording about it and sell it through an automated system. In that way you can help thousands by your solution.

6. Start your expert website.
The most successful consultants have a website that immediately offers a free material for an e-mail address. It shows all the available products and services that can be purchased by a credit card. Beside all these, it builds trust by blog posts and video materials.

The expert story appears in a highlighted space on the website because this is why people start to feel attached to you. You have to suggest that *"I had been in your shoes but with long and steady work I managed to solve the problem."*

Your website should have a marketing approach and each and every element should have its purpose: download of material, video view, and subscription or using any other functions.

7. Pass the solution to your potential customers.

When you have your solution ready and created your offer, the next tasks is to pass them to your target audience. There are many who do not dare doing a strong enough campaign because they are afraid of what other people might say about them. I saw an online course which was initiated by a weak campaign and it failed to fulfill the expectations that had been expected from it.

Remember that you cannot shout loud enough.

We receive more than 10.000 offers every single day that you cannot overemphasize by using free tools. Even if you make posts or stories daily… it will be simply not enough.

The best you can do is to start a Facebook campaign and you reproduce your expenses by your immediate offer that comes after your lead magnet. In that way you can build an e-mail list and a quality customer list for free that will help later to sell more offers.

8. Publish free contents.

Do not be afraid of the expression "FREE". Free videos ad blog posts will help to build trust and the expert status. If you succeed in building a well-functioning sales funnel and subscribers are coming for free, you can reach even thousands of interested potential customers.

By the provision of free materials in 12 months you can even build a list of interested potential customers that consists of 12.000 people.

9. Take hold of affiliate partners.

Partner marketing can bring you remarkable results as well. You find a partner who has a big and beautiful e-mail list of 20.000 people. He or she sends your lead magnet and approximately 800-1.000 new interested potential buyers are going to meet you. After subscription there will be around 10 people who purchase, which means $9.970 income regarding your $997 offer. You pay 30% commission to your affiliate partner, which means $2.991 and therefore $6.979 will remain in your own pocket.

Despite that, it is not its financial part what the best is about this. You will have 1.000 new subscribers. 150-200 among them is going to read your e-mails. Many of them will buy from you again and this means an enormous extra amount of profit.

10. Start the whole process again.

As the last step, I suggest that if you have a well-operating system, find another problem that your subscribers are suffering from and develop a new product to solve it. Send it through e-mail and the money will start moving to your account. ☺

I found the solution in the beginning of 2019 that I have used 14 times since then and I have optimized it.
I did a market research, I found the problem and I worked out the solution. I made a lead magnet from its most valuable part and I made an initial product and a main one from the remaining part.

Expert values you need to acquire

As an expert you must stand out of the crowd and you need to apply mindsets that make you move forward.

1. Be unique and distinguishable

The greatest mistake is when you copy a well known expert and you are not able to distinct yourself.
When I started back then, there were 2 or 3 marketing instructor experts who sold online courses… Nowadays, online courses start daily and there are many who apply the steps that I suggested and worked out.

Be unique and the market will recognize you.

Aim to give something new to your followers every single day. The more you help them the better you engrave your name in their minds. This is great because if you launch a new course to the market, they will pounce it up.

2.Endevour perfection but done is better.

Everyone would like to create perfection. But unfortunately, it does not exist. No matter how much you want it, you will not succeed. You must strive for completion in order to move forward as quickly as possible.

Each and every day you are waiting, you lose money.

The best is if you reach 80% of accomplishment and you launch your course immediately to the market. Meanwhile you can work on it so that it generates profit because this is what we live on.

3.Always overfulfil your customers' expectations.

Your customers expect you to deliver them what you had offered and what they had paid for. But nobody tells that it is forbidden to overfulfil their expectations.

How can you overfulfil expectations?

- extra gift courses, e-book materials
- Merci chocolate as a gift sent by post
- Unique T-shirt/mug with a logo sent by post
- Unexpected phone call after shopping

A kind phone call, a small gift or attention make you stand out immediately among your competitors. It is not a copyable technique, because only your customers get this experience.

4.Service comes first, then it is followed by everything else

As an expert you must SERVE your clients. Your business will not work if your clients feel that you are only after their money and you do not have the calling to the profession. As an expert you must have a mission that you have to make appear on your website.

An own example: "I am going to teach 110.000 entrepreneurs effective, online marketing strategies so that by applying them they can build a happier, and freer life as well as they can create a stable financial background for themselves…"

Write down your own mission statement shortly but comprehensibly. Pay careful attention on phrasing what you can help them…

5. Improve yourself continuously.

As a recognized expert you cannot afford leaning back. You must train yourself further because if you do not do that, you will fall behind. Self-improvement is inevitable but by your continuous renewal you can give even more to your followers and customers.

How can you improve yourself?
- Read books of your field and expertise. (English books, if possible.)
- Buy online trainings.
- Listen to professional Podcasts online.
- Watch professional YouTube videos continuously.
- Participate in all the events organized by your field of expertise.
- Find a mentor who is more ahead than where you are now.
- Buy expensive coaching and mentoring programs.

6. Build and nourish your relationships.

If you can, participate in offline events and on days of networking where you can meet new interested customers. Obtain as much followers on social media platforms as you just can and build separately segmented mailing lists on the basis of different topics.

Organize own events regularly and online webinars where you can be asked questions. You can use webinars for online sales as well because you can easily reach 10-15% of conversion by a good presentation.

Provide the opportunity of open house when your followers can call you and thus know you better. Be an available and ordinary person who can be looked up to and liked.

The 6 supporting pillars of successful expert business

I have been following the most successful experts and I found out the secret of their success. I observed the same pattern with most experts and I selected 6 activities from among them which they apply regularly.

I know that success depends on a thousand of things in business life but as an expert these 6 factors will have a significant effect on your results. Become the real master of these 6 activities and result will come by itself.

1. Content marketing and text writing

I observed with one of my American mentors, Jeff Walker, that he continuously communicates with the interested ones. He uses one particular content in many different formats, which can be a winning strategy for you as well.

Jeff Walker is the creator of Product Launch Formula System (PLF) makes video contents regularly which he publishes as a text as well as in his blog. This helps you to be searchable in Google and in YouTube as well.

Grant Cardone, Dean Graziosi and Russel Brunson communicate with no halt on Facebook, YouTube and Instagram. It is easy for them because a whole team work for them, but the way they communicate is an example to be followed. Follow them and pick up the techniques that make them millions of dollars.

The more you show up in front of the eyes of your target audience, the more customers you will have. This is similar to TV series, which are followed by millions week by week.

2. Public speech and presentation
It is a difficult genre but it is worth trying. The problem with public speech is that many people do not dare giving it because they are afraid. Those who have a go with it will improve, and the more presentations they give the more professional they become from time to time.

First, start small and give presentations to small groups of 5-10 people and if you become more brave you can give it a try in front of a constantly growing mass of people.

Imagine that you give a presentation on an event in front of 800 people. As you look round you stand riveted to earth. You step on the stage and become speechless... This is called stage fright. Everyone is struggling with it, but later this excitement will disappear slowly while giving one or two presentations like this. Do not misunderstand me, this is good because you take it seriously and it will be therefore more professional as you will prepare twice as much as others.

Look for professional conferences where you can give presentations, contact the organizers and sign up as a presenter. Many might think that it is difficult to get into an event as a presenter which is advertized by big names but in most cased you are welcomed.

3. Seminars and workshops
As an expert organize 1 day workshops regularly where you teach one particular topic. It is worth starting with smaller teams because then you will get a routine and after this you can have a go with bigger seminars.

You can do these online as well, which is a bit easier, as you will do the workshops or seminars in an online classroom by the help of Zoom software for instance. You can use any type of software, but you must give the opportunity to the audience to be able to ask questions from you.

There are strategies as well when the entrance fee covers only the expenses of the workshop. For example you rent a meeting room and you order coffee and cakes for the breaks. You are helped by 2-3 hostesses so as to do this smoothly. The costs of these start somewhere from $800, and the ceiling can be thousands of dollars if for example you would like to have the event in Hilton. A local offer is part of a strategy like this which makes the profit. The participants get an admission for $500 and you provide such an amount of knowledge in one day that 20 out of 100 attendees are going to buy your $997 offer.

4.Coaching programs:
This is going to be your high-ticket service which only few can afford, but this is not a problem because you will not have a burnout untimely. I will never understand coaches who are unable to change and work for peanuts.

In opposition to this it is so contrary that the best coaches can earn even $50.000 annually for the program. In these kind of programs there are approximately 50 participants and in many cases the target is to jump from the 1 million annual income to the 10 million.

People with ambition are willing to pay those coaches who have already reached what they themselves would also like to achieve.

5. Consultation and counseling:

It is another one to one job which cannot be scaled. You can sell an online course to thousands of people but you can have only 1 consultation at a time. It is important that it will work only if you ask for the right amount of payment for it.

My 2 hours consultation costs $500 and as an exchange for that price I provide such a professional knowledge that can create millions of income. Many of my clients gave the feedback that it was the consultation that helped them to clarify things that had to be done and the following day they had started building their system. It is my advice for you to give personal consultations and set its price in a way that not so many candidates would apply who engage the majority of your time.

One to one consultation is a great thing but because you can work with only one person at a time, if you take on too many of these, you will not have enough time for building other income generating systems.

6. Online marketing

By the help of marketing campaigns you can have such a breakthrough that you have not seen for years. There are many people who make false decisions and they spend nothing or only a minimum amount on marketing campaigns. Your expert business is going to be built up much quicker if you advertize and build your e-mail list. You must pay attention to generate a certain amount of profit that covers your costs of advertisement. In that way your campaign will finance itself and your e-mail list will grow for free.

Building expert funnels

In this chapter I will help you to plan and build your whole funnel that will help you to reach $120.000 annual income. It is important that customers do not know you yet. The best introduction is such an e-book/video that helps to solve a problem.

What is a funnel?

We call it a funnel but sometimes a value ladder because if we draw your products according to their values, you must see a beautiful, rising staircase. Your customers will move forward straight from your lead magnet to your priciest consultation. There will be some people who buy everything so as to acquire the maximum amount of knowledge. However the majority of the subscribers are going to stop and use only your free materials. There can be thousands of reasons why a customer does not step forward onto the next step but this is natural.

You must plan your product portfolio in a way that the free and initial product should give such a quality of knowledge which helps the customer solve a problem.

Yes, again I am writing about a problem, because the whole expert business is about problems and solutions. The expert who is unable to get his or her customers from point A to point B unfortunately will fall. It is a mistake to think that you are going to have an easy job. It is not easy to find out which problem is painful for most customers and whether the solution represents a greater value in their minds than the amount of money that you require for the solution. Value and providing value are the core tools of any expert.

How the funnel of a product increases your income

I accomplished an online marketing course in 2010 where I first heard about product funnel. At that time there had not been such professional funnels like the ones we use today. But there was one thing that I engraved well into my mind, that the bait product is the most important that had to be made accessible to people who were interested.

The product funnel is a good tool for increasing value because the customer first can request a free material, which does not require a high level of engagement. The second step is the initial product which is already a service to be paid. Therefore here the customers who pay and those who request the free material can be segmented. Those who have already opened their wallets can purchase from you later as well and this system has a great advantage.

Let's have a look at an own example:

16.500 registered for my free conference
1.900 purchased the video pack (initial product)
1.100 registered for my Academy (main product)
230 ordered smaller or a bit bigger jobs from me
52 paid for high ticket coaching

By the above mentioned ones, I reached an income above 1 million dollar. The question is that what level of income I would have reached if I only had advertized my products.

ANSWER: Approximately half of it as I would not have been able to communicate continuously and therefore sales had been harder.

Lead magnet: Gathering interested people on a production line
Lead magnet is FREE which helps reach the majority of your potential customers. There are many who are afraid of giving value in the form of their lead magnet, however the stingier you are with knowledge the less well it will work. The good lead magnet is eye-catching and it represents a value that will increase your self-brand as an expert.

Let the goal be to put together the best lead magnet in the world exceeding the expectations. My free mini courses brought a lot of customers because I pay attention on giving tremendous amount of value to those who gave me their trust.

Initial product: A great value product with a favorable price
It has one single function: to make a subscriber become a customer. In most cases we sell the initial product for such a low price that it is not really applicable to reach the income of 1 million. There is nothing wrong with that because its function is to convert subscribers to customers.

In rare cases a good initial product is also able to reproduce the expenses of your paid campaigns therefore in that case your customers will cost you nothing. A real goal can be to build a funnel like this. Let's agree that the initial product will segment the subscribers. It will help you find out who are the ones willing to buy from you and those who are just browsing around. You must concentrate on the customers; therefore the initial product is essential. I am going to write about this in detail in the following pages.

Main product: Your irrefutable offer

This is your basic product that you would like to sell. You must work out an irrefutable offer filled with extras and bonuses so that you can request the adequate price for it. Fill your package offer with extras then give a price with a discount. I have seen many successful examples built on this concept. Let's presume basically that your course is $997 and if you do not plan, you will discount its price by 30-50%. In contrast with that, it is much better if you add such value increasing elements to the package which will increase its price. An example: You prepare a package that worth $9.997 and you give a 90% individual discount from its price. As you do business with knowledge therefore making this offer depends on your creativity.

Profit maximization: Can I give it in a menu? or Can I give a bigger one?

It is the last step that creates extra profit. In many cases it does not include any extra cost because you offer an info product that way that does not involve any cost therefore has 100% profit content. I recommend you to offer this kind of product as UP-SELL, DOWN-SELL and BUMP-OFFER deals.

UP-SELL is a further offer of a small or a bigger value that is related to your original offer. DOWN-SELL is to be made appear to those who say 'no' to your UP-SELL offer. Finally, the BUMP-OFFER appears at the bottom of the form and can bring a tremendous amount of profit.

Average data of conversion:
UP-SELL: 10-25%
DOWN-SELL: 5-15%
BUMP-OFFER: 20-35%

Calculate the amount of money you lose if you do not use this.

EXAMPLE: 100 of your customers places 100 * 37$ that is $ 3.700. This is already a nice number but if we add the 25% BUMP-OFFER to it which is 25 * $27 then you increased your pure income by $675.

I observed this regarding my mentors' funnels. They offer a book for free but you are immediately given a 39$ BUMP-OFFER. After that a $297-$397 UP-SELL offer can come.

1# Prepare your free lead magnet

A free lead magnet is a product that is more valuable to a visitor than his or her e-mail address. They are glad to provide their names and e-mail addresses in order to receive a free material or a sample.
If you would like to attain visitors, this is the best online tool. Why? Because your potential customers are looking for a solution to a problem. You must help them with solving the problem by your lead magnet.

What is the function of a lead magnet?
The lead magnet has one single function, which is to create such positive visitors in mass who would like to know your applicable solution.

Thus the lead magnet is such a magnet that attracts visitors and requests their e-mail addresses. However, an e-mail address is a very personal stuff therefore there are many people who will not share it with everyone. Your task is to prepare such a lead magnet for which people are willing to provide their e-mail addresses.

E-mail address is important because then you can reach all the visitors and you can sell as well. You must calculate that one subscriber per month will worth $4 for you. So, if you have 1.000 subscribers (quality visitors) you can make a $4.000 income monthly by your e-mail list.

Your lead magnet therefore is the most important, because the better it is, the more quality visitors you will acquire and that way you are going to increase your monthly income.

What makes a lead magnet effective?

In the past few years I made minimum 100 lead magnets and I have realized what the secret of efficiency is, what makes it work and what does not.

1.)It solves a problem

If your lead magnet helps solving a problem or it provides such a value or knowledge that is desired, it will work and bring you thousands of visitors.

2.)It promises a tiny victory

Promise is one of the magical elements of the lead magnet. Certainly, not only promise must be made but the required solution has to be delivered. Briefly, you have to help to achieve something quickly and easily.

3.)Super specific

Do not make any general lead magnet that can help with anything. The best is if it offers an applicable solution specifically to a small problem. It converts better and brings more visitors.

4.)It can be consumed fast

PDF checklists work excellently because they can be consumed fast and used immediately. E-books work less well as people will not read them but they collect them in a folder on their computers.

5.)It is really valuable

The lead magnet should have as many representative and real values as possible. I teach my mentored ones to take the most valuable part of their offers and make it to be the lead magnet.

6.)It is instantly accessible
It is important that they should be able to download it immediately or to watch the video in a short period of time.

As you can see, I wrote it in 6 points above. You must pay attention to them while preparing the lead magnet but we have not examined yet what the best lead magnet would be for you.

The 10 most efficient lead magnet materials
It is time to have a look at the options you have. I will tell how easy or difficult it is to make a lead magnet. Choose the one you can make quickly.

1.)Downloadable e-book:
E-book is a brilliant lead magnet if you make it well. Visitors will not expect a 100 page book from you that they are never going to read. The best is the short one (5-10 pages long) and if you write it in a layout that leaves enough space between the lines which means that you write a sentence and press the "enter button" twice before you write another one.

2.)Video, video series:
I love videos because they maintain attention and they are sightful. Their other advantage is that people can connect to people. You can make the video recording in a way as if you were talking to a client sitting in front of you and you were presenting your solution right to him or to her. You will be given tons of advice in this book about how to make videos therefore if you grab your mobile and purchase a Boya M1 microphone, you will be able to record HD quality videos immediately. 10-15 years ago cameras were needed that cost millions in order to record videos. Nowadays your mobile is enough.

3.)Online mini-course:

Video series are even more striking than a single video because you can instruct in 4 videos, which is unique. There is only one thing that is better than that: LIVE webinar, but let's not run so fast forward. There will be 4 videos that you send via e-mail to visitors.

In the 1st video, it is worth presenting the problem in detail. The purpose of this video is to make the visitor feel that the problem requires an immediate solution.

In the 2nd video, tell your story in detail. Show them how you could solve the problem. The story of a hero works really well in this video (hero, obstacle, success).

In the 3rd video, offer the entire solution and show them the results that you and your clients achieved. This will raise interest in the solution.

In the 4th video, talk about what happens before and after the order. What kind of ability the customer will gain if he or she buys the product you offer.

Present all the bonuses and extras in detail. Use urging elements that encourage immediate purchase. This can be a deadline or the principle of limiting when only X number of customers can join.

4.)LIVE webinar:

This is the "Holy Grail", and believe me, I am not exaggerating. By each and every LIVE webinar you can make income. Approximately

15% of your audience will buy immediately during the webinar and in the 24 hours following it.

Your webinar presentation has key importance due to sales. In the first half of your presentation you must give the most knowledge/value as well as provide success stories and results that verify you. Following that, you must show the elements of your offer one by one. Place the elements of your offer on an imaginary table.

In the end of the webinar, "discount" the represented value. You remember, right? You pack your offer with bonuses that increase the represented value and then you will be able to give even 50-80% discount. In the end of your presentation show your offer again elements by elements and answer the questions in live. Deal with the occurring excuses and encourage the participants to make an instant decision by an extra gift.

5.)Online conference:
As for me, this was the thing that meant a real breakthrough. Surely, you have met the name of Online Marketing Summit in the beginning of 2019. I asked 40 experts to talk for 45-50 minutes and then I shared these interviews for 5 days. More than 16.000 entrepreneurs participated in this conference.

Online conference is one of the hardest lead magnets to build and it requires tremendous amount of time and money as an investment. I recommend this only to those who would like to TEAR IN the market. Do not worry, if this is your goal and you need help, contact me as I am continuously helping clients to build paid or free online conferences.

7.)Toolkit, checklist:

I intentionally left one of the most influential lead magnets, according to the statistics, to the end. The secret of it is that it can be consumed easily and the value that it represents. It is easy to make it and that is a great advantage in comparison with other lead magnet products. I recommend you to work out a solution to a problem that needs to be resolved and write the steps in the form of a checklist that can be ticked. They can print the checklist out which will encourage them in the realization.

2# Plan your initial product offer

Any online business is built on relationships and these relationships start when visitors provide their e-mail addresses. In the second step you have to differentiate the visitors who are only interested in the free lead magnets from the potential customers.

The best for this if you offer a deal between your free lead magnet and your most expensive product. Without that only few people are going to buy, however as you offer a deal with a fair price wallets are going to open immediately.

The initial product is one of the most important steps in the whole Buyer Value Optimization process. Only a portion of people who request the free lead magnet product will purchase.

What is an initial product?
An initial product is an offer that has been planned in a way that it converts as many visitors as possible to become a customer. It is such a good deal that most of the visitors cannot say "no" to it and therefore buy it instantly.

Its main purpose is not to make a profit but to bring you as many customers as possible and return the whole investment spent on advertisement. Many entrepreneurs set it even on a lower price so that they can acquire even more customers.

You can dominate the market if the majority of customers chose you. Certainly, apply the low pricing exclusively on the initial product, and offer your further deals for a higher price to your customers.

A Book as an Initial Product

It can be an ideal first product because of its relatively cheap price it does not require serious hesitation. The book is really useful for the customer and its representative price is enormous. And do not forget that there is no one who is going to throw a book away, but unfortunately they do that with business cards.

That way a book can also function as a business card. For example if you surprise a visitor with your book in a business meeting, you will have 50-60% greater chance to win him or her as your future customer. Between 2010 and 2014 I won hundreds of customers by giving them my online marketing book.

3 models that help you to sell your book effectively:

1.)Free book delivery offer

In this case you offer the book for free therefore there will be much more people who require it and you can increase the basket value by further offers. Do not be concerned about giving your book for free as your further deals will make the profit.

2.)Book sold for the original price (with free shipping)

This is the model we see most often when the book can be purchased with 1 or 2 gifts for a normal price. Free shipping can also be applied as a bonus. As everyone sells their books in that way therefore this is not really a good option and the sales of book is also expensive if we compare it with the other two models.

3.)Book offer with package pricing

If you would not like to give your book for free, choose this option. Work out package deals and offer 3 different kinds of prices. Make a cheap one, when only the book is given but bring the price of the second package close to it and fill the package with exciting bonuses. Make the third package disproportionately expensive and of course have some new bonuses in it, but be careful, not to give too sexy gifts. Make the customer feel that the second package deal is worth it so much that he or she does not want to leave it on the table but grab it immediately.

Online course as an initial product
This is better than the book as you do not have a fix expense like in the case of the book. You make a couple of hour course that the market usually sells for approximately $7-37 and offer it to the customer for a reasonable price. The sexier the deal is (many bonuses) the better it works.

In most cases I choose this one and 5% of the visitors, who I get for a $2-3 investment, will choose this deal. This way I spend $200 for which I get 100 visitors and from among them 5 will pay for the $37 course. This way the whole amount of the investment pays off and I can increase the daily cost of advertisement till 5 out of 100 visitors is buying my initial product.

Roughly the same system had been applied during the Online Marketing Summit Conferences and more than 1400 people bought the recordings of the presentations for $20.

3# Your irrefutable main product deal

The time has come to talk about your irrefutable deal. This product is basically 6 services that you offer to your customers for a higher price. The ones will buy this one who purchased your initial product as well.

Your main product should closely be related to your lead magnet and your initial product. Your customers should feel that as they move forward the funnel they get greater and more, complete and faster attendance and service.

How you should form your irrefutable deal?
Take the Digital Millionaire workbook in front of you and open it at the planner of the irrefutable deal. If you did not ask for the workbook, take a white sheet of paper and one blue + red + black color pen. As it is done, then start thinking about your deal and write down everything.

The best practice that I use is that I write down the elements of the deal with a blue color and after that their representative price with red in a bracket next to them. Number the elements with the black color so to mark which offer will include them.

For example you write down the idea of 3 or 4 e-books, check lists, videos, courses, audio materials, physical products, personal consulting and any other formats that you will be able to create. Following this, mark with number (1) what goes for the lead magnet, (2) is what the initial product is, (3) is the main product and (4) refers to the up-sells.

If you are done, you will see 10-15 elements which are going to be LEGO cubes in your case. You must build 4 Lego buildings and you have got to make sure that your package that contains the lead magnet and the initial product you pack are so valuable products that they would make even you buy them immediately.

Do not be afraid of giving the valuable parts for free or offer it for coins as the customer thinks in a way that if your free, downloadable material and your reasonably priced product helped so much, in your more expensive deals there are even more super valuable things you give.

In the mind of the customer every further deal from you will increase in value if you overfulfil the unexpected expectations. You must give more than they hope for and you are going to win them forever.

Get to know the Splintering techniques.
There are not so many who apply this, however this model is a gold mine. The first step is that you make a main product, full of useful things and you just simply slice a piece from it that you e.g. offer for free as a lead magnet. You offer another piece of it to the customer for a low price as an initial product. This is simple and great because you do not need to think much about your deal.

4# Let's maximize your profit by further deals

In the previous page we worked out the deals that convert visitors to customers who are willing to pay and then we make profit by an irrefutable offer. Now, we are going to increase your net profit by further deals. The secret of extra profit is that some of the customers would like to get everything you offer or they would like to solve their problem you offer a solution to faster.

How to make profit maximizations?
First of all, think over what is the thing that you had sold before. Further deals have to be attached to that as closely as possible. For example, if you sold a yoga mat after selling a yoga course and your yoga training in the 3rd step, you have to work out a deal that is closely related to that.

Actually, there is no rule regarding what should be offered here and on what price can work. Most of the profit increasing product/service can reach around 5-15% of conversion. The good news is that it is not the price why people do not buy. You can try to offer a very cheap deal and compare it with offering a normal or a high priced deal.

The result will be surprising. The profit will be similarly great except if you offer a High-Ticket deal. This will multiply your UP-SELL results ten times but you will be able to sell you high ticket service through a landing page. You should not sell on the UP-SELL site but offer a free 30-60 minutes talk instead and you do the sales there.

Bump offer: A low value stuff to the end of the form
You will love this solution because in an average 20-25% of the visitors will want this deal. So make sure that it is a very strong deal.

Do you remember that e.g. You make a 1 or 2 hour course for a specific topic that you do not sell separately but you place it in the end of the form. The representative price should be made visible and after that, give a huge discount.

Example: 2 hour Mandala Yoga Marterclass (value $97), but now you can have it for as much as $7.

As it is an info product it does not have any expense, so that way you can sell this deal even to 1000 customers. These deals work well because people pay attention on the details they provide while filling the form or the order, and they have already decided that they are going to buy from you anyway. While making the bump-offer, be careful to make the color of the offer 100% different from the colors of the landing page. My solution is that the background is orange and I frame the offer by a red dashed line.

UP-SELL: The extension, acceleration and increase of your offer
As you make your bump-offer deal, start planning your No.1 UP-SELL offer. This will be displayed on a separate sales landing page. In the first step, calculate the amount that your customer spent who has seen this offer. If your target group is price-sensitive, calculate 30-50% of the total price spent. Thus, if the total expense is $27 + $100 = $127, then price your UP-SELL offer between $27 and $57. Each customer makes purchases according to individual perspectives and some characteristic can be observed regarding these that we can use:

1.)"I need everything that can help."
Your precise and determined customers will buy the up-sell because they would like to know all the solutions and techniques. This book

is also a good example because most of the readers will only ask for the book and do not buy the course or any other supplementary material. This has a simple reason. They are not there yet, their problem is not painful enough, therefore they postpone the time of purchase. The majority will not buy courses from my later either, as they feel that this is not the way they are looking for.

HOWEVER, those who buy courses and workshops later and also register to the club membership, those are the ones who would like to achieve what I had achieved in the previous years. They know it well that if I could make it, I can help them achieve their goals.

2.)"I have to solve problems as quickly as possible."

The other half of the customers would like an immediate or at least a quicker solution, therefore they buy the UP-SELL as well. Imagine, if you have a toothache and all the dentistry offices are closed except the one in downtown. You will make a phone call and you are willing to pay even a higher amount if your painful problem can be solved quickly.

Speed is not that important in some cases but then you can offer e.g. an A'la cart service. Let's have a look at an example: You sell a course that is about making a website and approximately 10-15% of the customers will leave the task for you.

DOWN-SELL: A new offer that might interest him or her
The customers who asked for your main deal, but they did not ask for the UP-SELL should be offered another, cheaper deal. Here the goal is to convince them to buy even if we make less profit.

There is a down-sell tactics which I do not recommend you, and this is not to decrease the price of the UP-SELL, therefore devaluate it. Imagine yourself in the shoe of the customer, how would you feel if the $997 deal was offered for $97 2 second later?

Instead, examine the original problem that made the customer pay and offer them a completely new deal that is in relation with the original problem. Pricing is a very important issue regarding this deal. By all means, offer it for a more favorable price that the UP-SELL deal and if necessary, offer them the opportunity of installment.

CROSS-SELL: Completely different offer
You must offer a completely different deal here than previously. It does not need to be related to any other deals but a brand-new topic which is exciting enough for the customer to swoop the deal. The best example to this is when you are offered chips and soda to your burger in a fast food restaurant.

Let's plan your $20.000 income
The unachievable this amount may seem, we shall make it together. You must understand that until you concentrate on selling your time, it will be impossible.

The problem with enterprises which charge hourly is that they are cannot be scaled. This means that you can serve maximum 10-20 clients each and every month. In contrast with that, if you have a professional automatic system, you can help thousands of customers and solve their problems.

Let's compare 2 businesses:

1.)A business with an hourly fee:
You can work 2 or 3 clients a day in order not to get tired utterly. These couple of clients can move forward continuously but unfortunately you, as an expert will burn out within a few years. You work with 20 clients and you spend around 2-3 hours with everyone. If you work below price then you can earn $20 * 60 hours = $ 1.200 but you burn out and will hate your profession.

2.)Automated business:
Here you can help even 100 clients with a single online course and the 10 bests from among them are going to pay for your high-priced High-Ticket consultation. This means that next to your 100 * $97 offer, your 10 * $997 deal is also coming. This is $ 19.670 per month. You can gain 10x if you work with a smart, automated system and you can change 10x customers' lives. This is a real WIN-WIN business.

1.)Even an initial product is enough for $2.700 income monthly

Let's say that you do nothing else but you make your initial product.

Let's price it between $7 and $27 and reach 1.000 visitors. Approximately 10% of them will ask for your next (highly representative-priced) irresistible offer. That way math shows that you will end up with $27 * 100 customers = $2.700 income. Certainly, you are going to have expenses as well but the good news is that you will also have 100 new customers per month.

2.)Offer a $37 BUMP-OFFER deal

This is a small step that takes 5-10 minutes to make and in return it is going to increase your profit that your system produces. Calculating with 20-25% average conversion you are going to see that 25 out of 100 customer will ask for that "ask for this for a better price as well" deal that occurs in the end of your form.

Math will go like this: $37 * 25 customers = $925 and we add to that the $2.700 income as well from point 1. That way we already have reached $3.625 by 2 offers.

3.)Make an irrefutable main product deal

This is going to be the more difficult step because we will boost your main offer. I will cover the irrefutable deal in detail, in another chapter, later in the book. Briefly, the point is that add 6-8 bonuses that you can give the client in a way that it does not cost you anything.

Math: $997 * 10 customers = $9.970 to which we add the income in point 2 ($3.625) and that way we have $13.595 income, which is quite a nice monthly wage for you.

4)Offer profit maximizing deals

This is the cherry on top. From among those who buy your main deal there will be approximately 2 or 3 who purchase this one as well. The price/representative value has to be very powerful here. Customers have to feel in a way that if they do not request the 100% complete solution, they will regret not buying it.

Let's say that we accommodate an UP-SELL deal to your irrefutable $997 offer that costs only $297. This can be requested even by 15% of them but those who do not want it should get another completely different deal that costs only around $197. It can also work if a higher-priced, even $497 offer is proposed in which they can have a consultation personally with you.

The aim here is to make $997 profit in a way that costs $0. This is the secret of automated systems and this is what every expert, consultant and coach should use.

As you can see, reaching the monthly income is easier than you would imagine. If it is build logically and the deals are connected to each other, the system will work. The more experienced you become in making videos and writing texts, the more customers will spend money on your services and that way, the more you are going to help to solve their problems.

3.) The Toolkit of Digital Millionaires

1.) The toolkit of the digital millionaires

Every online business needs tools that enable you to make your online courses be able to communicate to your visitors as well as be capable of making LIVE presentations.

You will need online tools to record online videos, to make online courses and graphics that are needed. I collected everything in this chapter that you will need.

What kind of tools will you need?

You will need hardware and software for your work. You will get to know the devices that I use in the following pages.

Kajabi: All software in one tool

You can choose from among plenty of software but none of them contains all the tools you would need. Wordpress is also a good choice but if you buy all the software for it, you could also have paid for the monthly fee of Kajabi approximately.

One of the great advantages of Kajabi is that it can be used really easily and this single software is enough to build your business. I have been using it since 2015 and I would never exchange it to any other software. You can make your own online course and Kajabi is capable of selling your deals really efficiently.

You can build sales funnels by the help of Pipelines, a few clicks and you can make LIVE or evergreen webinars.

Microphones: Why is it important to buy a microphone?
As for the videos the most important is the quality of voice but you will need a proper microphone. This does not mean that you should buy an expensive one. More and more low-priced microphones can be purchased on the markets that are almost as good as the expensive ones.

Camera: Your mobile phone from your pocket is enough… (Min. HD)
In the initial phase I do not recommend you to buy expensive camera. Simply use your mobile. It is practical, always at hand and most of the mobiles nowadays can record HD quality videos. Pay attention to have enough free space storage on your mobile phone and the lens cleaned. The most professional videos are made by DSLR camera. I have a CANON 5D IV and it can record an excellent quality. I do not recommend it in the initial period because of its price.

Lights: Natural light or softbox lamp
The best could be natural light if you record videos outside. Its great advantage is that you do not need other light sources. You can record the videos by yourself using a stand but if you have a cameraman, you can use a reflecting screen as well.

While recording indoor videos you will need lights. The perfect light set includes 3 softboxes. You can use a fourth light which lights you from above. I recommend you adjustable led softbox because that way luminance and temperature of light can be adjusted easily.

Software you have to work with later

Kajabi is going to be the most important software but you will need some other ones as well that you use for making your online courses. I will also recommend some software for editing your video that you can make professional videos with in a simple way.

A part of the software is for free, the other half of them will charge you monthly or they can be purchased for a single payment. I will notify you about every single software if they are not important, so that you can avoid unnecessary spending.

Presentation software for making your presentations

You can make presentations the easiest way if you create the presentations in Keynote or in PowerPoint and you record them by using an external microphone.

If you use Mac, the best choice is Keynote as you receive it for free with your computer. Keynote is capable of many functions and you can find really beautiful templates for presentations in it.

Powerpoint or Prezi online can be suitable for PC. The only condition is that the presentation software should be able to record presentations in video format.

The only thing for you to do is to make your presentations, you start the recording and you also record your voice as you are moving forward with the slides. I record all my courses that way, so that my customers can easily learn from me.

Which microphone should I chose for recording my videos?

In the following pages I am going to talk about microphones and I hope that you will be able to choose the right one. I have completed already many online courses and there were some which were really bad qualities. In one of them for instance a recording of a Zoom meeting was shared which had been recorded by an embedded microphone and I could not hear anything of what they said.

Pay attention to the quality of the sound as it cannot be improved later

One of the basic rules while making online courses that the sound should be high quality. Some years ago these devices were quite expensive nowadays you can purchase better quality of microphones for a reasonable price.

The quality of sound is important because you cannot improve it later. If the quality of sound is bad your whole recording can be thrown into the trash. If the sound quality is bad, your good presentation is in vain. Sound recording is one of the most important steps in the mentoring program.

Many times the sound is a good quality but it is ruined by other noises. Before recording a video, you have to make sure that there are no other noises in your environment that would ruin your recording.

In the following page I recommend the Boya BY-M1 microphone because you can buy it for a reasonable price and it can record a great quality of sound. I will also tell you about the Blue Yeti microphone, which is already a professional studio microphone, and

I will also mention the microphone of Rode, which can be a perfect choice in combination with a DSLR camera.

Boya BY-M1 : Entry lavalier microphone

This is one of my favorite microphones that I use if I make an external recording on a weekly basis. Due to the 6 meters long cable it can be used for any kind of recording.

Amazon price: $19.50

Blue Yeti and Snowball: Quality studio table microphone

Its main advantage is that it is a USB microphone. There is no need for an external sound card for it and despite of that it can record a professional quality of sound. Yeti can do that in an outstanding quality whereas Snowball unfortunately in a lower quality but I recommend both of them.
Yeti price: $129
Snowball price: $69

Rode VideoMic Pro+ : A microphone that can be fixed on a camera

This is an excellent microphone that you can set on a camera as well as on a digital camera. This is a pistol microphone that records the sound in front of it in a great quality.

Amazon price: $260-$280

Røde Wireless Go: Wireless Quality Microphone

I left a wireless microphone for the end as well. The main advantage of it is that it is comfortable and you can move freely.

What kind of camera should I use to record the videos?

You will have to make a lot of videos for the online courses so let's overview what you will need. When choosing your camera you must take many aspects into consideration as they are essential:

1.)HD quality camera: In order to provide an excellent quality in marketing and in the online courses, we will need HD quality. This is a basic setting in most of the mobile phones.

2)Big storage space: For the storage of HD and 4K videos big size storage space is needed. There are mobiles with extendible storage space but most of them are fixed. I recommend you to empty at least 32-64 GB space on your mobile to have enough storage.

Choosing the camera is an important step
You have to define in advance what kind of videos you are going to record and also the number of them. There are cameras which can record maximum 30 to 40 minutes and their batteries go off. In contrast with professional cameras which are able to record even 3 to 4 hours.

It is also an important aspect how difficult it is to use the camera. For instance it is as easy as a pie to record videos by a mobile phone whereas setting up a DSLR camera requires serious preparation. First time it was also difficult for me to set my Canon 5D Mark IV. camera in a way to make similarly great videos as with the mobile phone.

It is not negligible either how much you spend on a camera. Choose the best value and price ratio.

Mobile: Most of the mobile phones are capable of recording HD

It is worth recording the videos with your mobile first. It is easy to handle it and you can see the recording immediately. Actually, most of the mobiles are capable of recording 4K quality but I recommend you the HD quality. You can buy accessories to your mobile which enable you to develop the quality of the picture and the sound as well as enlarge or reduce the pictures by the help of specific lenses. A few years ago I bought a Moment Wide Lens and it was enough to set my mobile 20-30 cm far. You can find many useful devices on the Internet.

GoPro: It is tiny and you can take it with you to record videos at any time

This action camera is a great device, as its small size makes it possible for you to record great quality videos anywhere. The newest GoPro can record videos in 4K already. I loved working with this camera because it is easy to handle and the recordings can be copied to my computer.

Logitech c920 : HD webcamera with professional video recording

There are many people who are afraid of the quality that they can make by a webcamera but nowadays you can record a great quality with them. I record the units of my online courses by webcamera with a green canvas in the background. In that way I am able to make the recordings by Green Screen technology. Logitech already produces 4K quality webcameras so if you set perfect quality as a goal then this can be a great choice.

DSLR : Movie quality video recording

I intentionally left DSLR cameras for the end because it is more difficult to work with them, but in return you can make the best possible quality by using them. I work with a Canon 5D Mark IV and I record professional 4K videos. You will need a stand, lights, microphone, objective and a good background apart from having the DSLR camera. When you watch a few videos on YouTube, it can clearly be seen which one of them had been recorded by a DSLR camera and which is the one taken by a mobile phone. The greatest advantage of DSLR is that it obscures the background and it provides a professional quality of video recordings.

Its negative side is its price. The objective and all the equipments cost more than all the other cameras. If the higher cost is not a problem for you I recommend you to record all the videos by DSLR definitely.

Most of the well-known American marketing experts without exception use professional DSLR cameras to record their marketing videos and online course presentations. Certainly, you will not need immediately the most professional technology, start with your mobile phone and then later your can change for DSLR technology.

Do not forget that if the quality of the video recordings is poor, the participant will think that your online course is not good either therefore you will end up with poor results.

Natural light or softbox? Which one should you choose?

For making great quality, good lights are required. Natural light is the best that you can use while making videos outside. This will not cost you anything and if you record the videos in the right time their pictorialness is going to be harmonious. Softbox is an internal device from which 2 or 3 are needed in order to have the required quality.

Softbox can be led or halogen technology but it is important to light yourself from two sides and there should be a background illumination as well that juggles the shadows away. Now I am going to help you to choose the right type of lighting so that your videos can look as professional as possible.

Make provision for the right type of lighting
If there is no appropriate illumination, the video will be dark and you will be seen less clearly as well. This is why lighting has critical importance in case of each and every video you are going to make in the future. My first videos had been recorded outside because I did not have the right lighting equipment at that time. Later, when I had the money to buy lights, I instantly purchased 3 pieces of softbox lamps so that I could also make great quality videos in my office. You can buy the lights for your videos for a relatively low price so no severe amount is needed to be invested for making professional quality of recordings.

Test the quality of recording before making each and every video. After making the video check the quality of the recordings and if it is needed, record them again for the sake of the better quality.

Record outside and use natural light

For beginners the best opportunity is sunlight as you do not need to buy anything and the recording will still be perfect. You must pay attention to the fact that there will be one or two hours in the morning and in the evening period when sunlight is going to be appropriate for the video. There are basic mistakes that you must avoid, one of them is when the sun is in front of you and you blink strongly due to the strong light and that can be seen on the video.

Another common mistake is when the sun is behind you and you are in semi-darkness. This can happen if you make the recording in the wrong time. Check the concepts of golden hour and blue hour. These are the hours each and every day when you can record videos without making the above mentioned mistakes. While making the recordings outdoor you need to be very attentive concerning the quality of sound, therefore use devices that reduce outdoor noises. These noises can ruin your videos because there is no use if the pictorialness is perfect but the audio part is messed up.

What is softbox and how to use it? (3 softbox)

We know many kinds of softbox but their typical feature is that there are 4 to 6 or 8 lights lighting on a stand and in a special frame. In front of the lamps there is a white layer which dims the lights and that way it is able to light greater spaces perfectly.

2 or 3 softbox is needed for recording the videos, one will illuminate you from the left, the other is from the right and the third light abolishes the shadow appearing behind your back. Actually, if you pay attention to this, you cannot make many more mistakes. Softboxes can be fine tuned in most cases so if the light is too strong you can reduce the intensity. It is important to pay attention not to

make the lighting either too strong or too weak. You must find the balance that will make the recording perfect. Lots of practice is needed in order to be able to do that, so your first videos are not going to be the best but you will learn a lot.

Newer led panels with greater illuminating power

There are already new LED lights as well which you can use in softbox and on own led stands. Led lights can be more customized, their power as well as their temperature of light can be regulated. LED can make cold and warm lights as well which will enable you to create an individual pictorialness in the background. LED does not blind so much if it is set in the right way and consumes little electricity.

Ring light: Individual appearance with round light

There will be many who are going to choose this lamp because it is simple and lights only and exclusively you. It can create a wonderful pictorialness in a way that everything is darker around you but you are lit perfectly. I saw many videos that had been made by using this device and they were all perfect without any exception. Look for it on the Internet and choose a medium priced light that you can use for making professional videos.

I helped you above with choosing the right type of light but I ask you to check them on YouTube and make your decision on the basis of that.

5 software that helped me build my own business

I have been building online businesses that sell knowledge since 2015. I needed more software with which I can make pictures and videos and at the same time I can sell the knowledge that is shared in my courses. Now I am going to share these software with you that helped me build a 100 million business in the past years.

Canva.com: Pictures, covers and illustrations
You will need graphic elements on your website and for your online courses. You can make these the easiest way if you use the right tool. Canva is a software that assists you with making professional graphic elements by providing previously prepared graphics. It is easy to handle and it can even be used for free. It is worth signing up for it as that way you can use more graphics.

Canva is a graphic designer tool. You can even make your ads as well as the graphic elements of your online courses in a professional quality. Many other similar software can be found on the Internet, try some of them and chose the one you like the most.
If you can use Photoshop, you will not need Canva. Using Photoshop is a lot harder therefore I recommend Canva for the beginners. Graphic design is one of the most important steps while making online courses. It must be unique, so good quality and designs are the right tools to make it.

OBS/Ecamm Live: For LIVE and recording videos
You can use these software to record videos and making LIVE videos. They handle more cameras and you will be able to divide your table so you can give presentations as well.
I use Ecamm-LIVE software to record my online courses and keep continuous contact with my customers. You can use your DSLR

camera as well with this software and that way you can give 4K quality presentations on Facebook, on YouTube or on other social media platforms.

Its main advantage is that you can invite guests to the LIVE stream via Skype call and you can easily share the comments during the time of the live show. The new version is able to make Green Screen videos so that way you can broadcast Facebook lives with a unique background.

Vidello Create: For making creative ads
I am sure that you have already seen ads on Facebook that had texts below and above the videos. These video ads are very good because you can make better converting campaigns with them. Try this software and you will be able to make professional videos with them.

Its other advantage is that you can use pictures and videos from the Internet for free so you can make your own videos more colorful and fascinating. The software offers background music so that way you will be able to make more exciting videos.

Teamweek.com: Plan precisely for 2 or 3 months
The most important production device as you can create daily and monthly plans in this software. If you work with a bigger team, you can give a distinct task to everyone and you can follow the completion of the delegated tasks. I plan minimum four weeks in advance and I exactly now the tasks of each and every day.

As an entrepreneur you must plan your tasks in advance as this is how you can be more productive. The more you use this software the greater results you will reach. There are many of these type of software, try more of them and use the one you feel the most comfortable with.

Do not forget that if you do not plan each and every hour, someone else will schedule your time. Set deadlines and define the tasks of your daily work. Set milestones and try to reach the goal quicker that you targeted when you founded your own business.

Do the tasks defined in the software in time and do not procrastinate. If you act that way, your marketing materials will be done in time as well as the presentations of your online course and all the other tools that you will need.

Planning and realization are the secret to build a successful indeed Knowledge Commerce. This tool has been helping my work for years now and by the help of it I procrastinated less. I achieved much more than my rivals.

Kajabi: The all-in-one software
The heart and soul of my business is Kajabi. I made my funnels, my e-mail campaigns, my website, my webinars and my online courses in this software. Everything can be found in it that you will need and in most cases there is no need for any other external software. Kajabi is improving continuously and it supports your work with new functions.

In some pages I am going to show you the functions of Kajabi and I hope that by its assistance you will also build a successful and gradually growing business.

If you would not like to work with Kajabi, you will need to work harder as you have to build a WordPress website and to rent minimum 8-10 external software. You will need to link these in order to be able to build an automated online business. Zapier can help you in that but it is going to be a much greater amount of work than with Kajabi.

I started using Kajabi in 2015 and as a founding member I have been supporting the developers with my ideas. Currently, Kajabi is the only software that includes everything that a Knowledge Commerce entrepreneur needs. I love this software because it is easy to handle and a funnel can be made in seconds which would be several weeks of work by a WordPress.

Presentation software for making presentations

You can make the presentations for the online course the easiest way if you make presentations and record them as you project them. In the following, I am going to help you make professional presentations and share all my experience with you.

Before you install the application of making presentations
You must do a research on what your target group needs before you make the course. When you are aware of that, you must work out a solution to the problem. After the solution, the testing of the course can come when you write down the titles of the modules and the presentations. After the planning you can start making the presentations and when you are done you can transform it to a video by the help of a microphone. We have already discussed the microphone but have not mention the presentation software yet.

In the following I am going to show you two software that will help you to record these presentations. It does not matter at all whether you have a PC or a Mac computer. I use Keynote program on Mac which enables me to make professional presentations. If someone uses Windows, I recommend PowerPoint as you can make approximately the same quality with it.

You will need pictures for the presentations as well which you can download for free from the relevant sites. If you download pictures from Google browser you can violate the rights of others so I ask you not to do that.

MAC: Keynote as an application for making presentations

If you use an Apple computer you can download Keynote application for completely free. You can make presentations on the basis of topics which are previously prepared in the program. This program is able to record your voice while you are moving forward and you can export it as a video. The use of software is really simple so there is no need for any kind of previous education for it. The design is easily adjustable. You can insert videos and your own pictures. In the past few years my courses have been made in this software in 100%. I prepared my presentations and then recorded my lectures. As none of them will require editing or any kind of rework later, therefore you can make presentations really fast by using it. I recommend you to download it from Apple store and start using this fantastic software.

PC: PowerPoint presentation making application

If you are working on a PC, PowerPoint is the right tool for you. Similarly to Keynote software you can make your presentation here as well, after that you can record it, and then save it as a video. With both operation systems the process is the same. You create 10-12 presentations according to the topics of the onlinc course and you make them in the form of presentations.

If you would like to use web presentation software, prezi.com is the best tool for you. By Prezi you can make online presentations.

Freepik: Procurement of free pictures and illustrations

You will use pictures and illustrations in presentations so it is worth procuring them from websites where you can download free images. One of these that I use is Freepik.com, but I recommend Pixbay.com as well. Whatever you chose from among them, you will win as you can choose from among many quality pictures.

The secrets of making impressive presentations
In this blog, I promise that I will share secrets with you that make your presentation more successful. The truth is that pictures and designs are very important, but what are more important than them are: the message and the value you provide.

We do not fill impressive slides with texts and we teach new things in an easily comprehensible way to the audience. Make sure you use your logo and the colors of your brand constantly in your presentation.

The secret of effective presentation is your own self. Your presentation can be very impressive, but what you say and the way you present it is more important. The best presenters do not flood all the information to the audience but rather trigger their thoughts.

Video lecture from an accomplished presentation
Most software are able to record your voice while you move forward with your presentation. Later you can export this recording with the picture and the sound.

Kajabi: The heart and soul of your online business

As far as I am aware of myself I have been continuously searching and looking for those solutions that make my work easier. I have tested plenty of this kind of software, but there are two of them that I am using constantly. One of them is Kajabi, the other one is Adespresso advertisement managing program.

I would like to show you the advantages of Kajabi so that you will be able to make a good decision. I am well aware that WordPress is free but you need to buy many other software in order to be able to build the same system as with Kajabi.

I had made a calculation, and I found that in many cases while building a WordPress system a higher monthly fee has to be paid than with Kajabi.

In the following pages I am going to show you what Kajabi includes and I will leave the decision onto you whether you put together a complicated and, in many cases, an incompatible system or you choose a reliable, ready-to-use software that is what you just need.

Why should you choose Kajabi software?

I have been using this software for 5 years now and I remember when in 2015 I started making my first online course. I felt that this software is a perfect fit for making any task that is ahead. Anything I made worked perfectly and I could present it in an exquisite quality to my clients. Therefore I definitely recommend you to try Kajabi software for 28 days. I made a special link which you can use for requesting a 28 day trial opportunity. Type this link below in your browser.

28 DAYS TRIAL: http://bit.ly/2UBdinx

The most important functions of Kajabi

In the following I am going to summarize the two functions that you can rely on while starting a successful online business. Its previous functions are continuously expanded. Certainly, this is not a Kajabi manual therefore excuse me that I am going to write down only the essences.

1.)Making a website, a blog and a landing page
You can make your website in the system, start a blog or make an effective landing page. The planner creates pages that easy-to-use and optimized for professional conversion. You will not need WordPress either as you can make a great website in the software easily by a few clicks. Long time ago I created sales pages but they did not produced the fantastic results that I reached by the ones that I made by Kajabi. The builder consists of blocks and fitted functions.

2.)Online course and subscription system
This is the most exciting part of the software as you can create different kind of online courses really easily. More pre-prepared so called Blueprints are available that you can use by a click then you can easily personalize them while creating your online course. I must mention the function of the subscription system. If you upload online courses and you would like to sell them in subscription system this fantastic software will offer you a solution to that as well.

3.)Funnels and offers
Surely you know funnels but you will not be able to create them so easily in any other software. First, you make your offer in which you can include more online courses. In the next step, you make your sales funnel (PIPELINE), you rewrite the text and upload the videos.

You can move forward fast and the end result is so professional as if you had spent millions on the assistance of an expert.

You can choose from among many different types of funnels therefore I am certain that you find the one that suits best to your strategy. Such a Pipeline includes landing pages, forms, the automated e-mail series as well as the sales system. You do not have to think about how you should build the system as you receive a well thought over and tested system after a few clicks.

4.)E-mail marketing and automatization

I am really into the e-mail marketing function of the software because it is simple and I can send my offer efficiently to my visitors. Due to CRM segmentation I can send the right message to everyone on the right time. The system is capable of sending automated e-mail series as well as forwarding single Broadcast newsletters. The e-mail constructor has improved a lot in the previous years and now many different professional designs can be selected. Certainly, it can also be linked with external e-mail marketing software in case you need a unique solution, but the e-mail marketing system will support you extensively. You can send the e-mail to only those who have not read them yet. You can start automated e-mail series after subscription and you can halt them as well automatically as the customer purchases your offer. You can start or halt automated e-mail processes in each and every stage.

4.) LIVE and recorded online events

This is one of the best webinar software that I have ever tried as we can make LIVE webinars in Kajabi by integrating Zoom and YouTube. The advantage of this is that you can present your offer in live and much more people will purchase in the end of your presentation.

In the beginning of 2019 I made my Online Marketing Summit event by Kajabi software where there were more than 16.000 participants. You are able to give previously recorded, so called evergreen presentations. Presentations can be played daily, in every hour or minute. This is one of the most powerful marketing tools which can help you to make profit.

6.)CRM system and segmentation
A professional CRM system is part of the whole system as well, where the segmentation of subscribers is as easy as pie. You can create segments of subscribers who have never purchased from you before or who have already done that. You can differentiate the customers on the basis of purchased courses. Imagine the amount of success you could reach by the application of an automated, segmented sales system. CRM stores the data about the exact purchase of the customer and therefore in the next step it makes an offer on the basis of the stored data.

7.) Kajabi mobile application
The greatest technical innovation of recent times is the mobile application that is available in the iOS as well as in Android devices. The customer installs the mobile application and can join your course through a mobile phone instantly. There will be no idleness, when he or she is waiting for something can just open the application and learn. The mobile phone is the most important device in people's lives so if you would like to achieve great results, you can do that by using the mobile application of Kajabi.

Why Kajabi is better than any other similar solution?
We have already discussed that this system can be done by WordPress, but you spend approximately as much as the monthly fee

of Kajabi. This is going to be a system that basically had not been created for this purpose therefore is not reliable. You can do it that way but it is not easy for this reason, therefore using the right tool would be logical in order to build up your Knowledge Commerce business.

Kajabihero: The path from $1.000 to $100.000
I have great news because if you use Kajabi, you will take part in an internal program. The precondition of this is that all your sales should happen within the software. Kajabi rewards you with different types of awards when you reach a certain amount of income and this will encourage you to move forward even faster. I currently reached a $100.000 level of income with no more than a subscription system. The next level is going to be $250.000 when the company encourages by new presents.

4.) Let's Plan Your First

Online Course

4.) Let's Plan Your First Online Course

Finally, the moment has come when we are going to work on your first online course. I will give all the information to your hand that you need in order to distribute your message to thousands of people and help them that way. In the first step, we are going to define your target audience and after that we are going to make them receive one of your offers.

Thematic and Strategic Planning of an Online Course

It is important for you to understand that the most successful online courses are those which are planned point by point. It provides a solution to the problem of the customer and focuses on the achievement of the great results. It encourages customers to act and therefore thousands of satisfied customers are going to buy from you in the following years.

Work out the profile of your ideal customer (Avatar)

Your ideal customer is the person who has the problem to that knowledge and wisdom means the solution to. You have to know your customer in order to offer him/her the right solution in the right form and place. By doing market research you have to find out all the information that you will need for building your strategy. In the ideal customer profile you need to summarize the demographic data, the challenges and problems as well as the goals of your customer. All of these will show what your customer finds valuable enough to be willing to pay for it.

Find the problem that makes your customers suffer

Customers fight with many problems day by day, the winner is the one who explores these problems and can offer effective solutions for solving them. I saw many courses that could not be sold on the market, which had a simple reason. They did not focus on the problems of the customer but the maker of the course decided what kind of problem he or she was going to solve.

The online courses that solve a real problem, encourage action and represent value are marketable. The intensification of the problem is one of the stepping stones in your marketing business. There are many who halt at this point but this is followed by the effective solution that puts an end to the problem.

Assemble the syllabus on the basis of the market research

You need to speak the language of the customer. You must do a market research in which the visitors can write about their problems in their own words. Later the titles of my online courses will be composed of these words. After that the customers will feel that it addressed to them and they will not hesitate whether to buy the courses.

Make the questionnaire as simple as you can and if it is possible do not ask more than 2 or 3 questions. Offer options of free word choices so as to make customers write down their problems with their own words. You can not only use these in your online courses but also you must use them in the text of your marketing campaigns.

If you act that way, your course will be marketable.

Work out the tasks for the end of the modules

Make a video for the end of your each and every modules in which you give tasks and challenges to the participants. The tasks will encourage them to act and that way you make them step on the path of the solution. The challenge should not be easy but neither too hard because you scare them away from realization.

Create your private study group on Facebook
You cannot sell Facebook groups as products but as a part of an offer they are an excellent opportunity to build a community. Private exclusive groups created for the customers offer such a support that they will not be able to get anywhere else.

Be present in the Facebook group continuously and offer help to your customers so as to strengthen the relationship with them. It will not be an easy job but by the end you will have your own community and many of them will buy from you again. Community is one of the strongest elements of this new business model. The members of the group are going to help each other, so after a while much less energy is needed to moderate the group and to answer the questions.

Your online course is going to be really successful if you plan everything in detail and you build your business on the basis of the plan continuously. Month by month you will reach newer and newer customers and apart from the stable financial income you create a community which supports you and counts on your help.

Scheduling the Courses and Building up the Presentations

In the following, I would like to help you to be able to schedule the online courses appropriately and enable you to make presentations that your customers will watch favorably. The more satisfied your customers are the more certain is that they are going to buy from you again. You must build trust and encourage your customers to achieve results.

Your online course should be at least 5 weeks long
It should not be too short because then it does not seem as valuable but it should not be too long either because then your customers will think that they will not be able to accomplish your course.
There are exceptions but I ask you to consider 5 weeks as a basis and if it is needed you can diverge from that. 5 weeks is easily accomplishable but in contrast with that a 6 months course seems much harder. Provide a 30 day warranty, so that way those who finish your course, up until the fourth week, will not claim their money back.

Open the modules and drip the course material week by week, slowly and step by step
Open the modules slowly week by week so that your followers can move forward slowly. Most people do not have much time off. If a couple of hours learning is enough for the course, much more people will buy it and accomplish it. In comparison with that if the customer after the purchase gets a 100 hour long online course, he or she will lose all the enthusiasm even to start your course, this is why I really like this so called "Dripping training technique", when we send learning materials on a weekly basis.

The weekly material should not be longer than two or two and a half hour.

You make the best decision if the length of the weekly material is approximately 2 hours. In that case, the participant does not feel that he or she will not have enough time to finish the weekly sessions. Try to share the knowledge that is needed right then during that short period of time. The more concise and prompt form you can make to share your knowledge, the more people will accomplish your course and that way you can reach a great breakthrough and success with more people. Here your presentations will have a significant role which has been discussed in the previous pages. If your presentation is constructed well, you can pass relevant information in a short time so you can encourage the participants of the course to act.

Choose the format of the presentation
You can make the presentations of your course in 4 different types of format. Let's have a look at them one by one how they differ and how you can use them in order to achieve the greatest result.

1.)Screenshot: The simplest solution is to make a screenshot as with this one you can record what you are doing right on the screen. While you talk you lead the attention of the participants and you present them those steps that they need in practice. It is an effective way of presentation because the participant watches the video and after that they can achieve the same that you have already been able to reach. There are many of these types of software on the market but I ask you to try as many as you can and for recording use the one that produces simple and great quality.

2.) Video with a head speaker:
This is a bit more difficult video to make as you will need a background, light and also yourself. You start the recording and share the information that you would like to distribute to the participants. If you have stage fright, practice as much as you can, so after a while you will feel that you are less and less tensed. You need to use this type of video in your presentations as well as in your marketing. One of the most important elements of sales funnels are the videos in which you share information and incentives to make potential customers buy from you. Learn how to make this type of video as it can remarkably increase your sales.

3.) Interview:
Ask experts for giving professional interviews. These interviews will help to make you appear more reliable and to be able to share valuable information with your students. Make interviews in which you mention the topics of your course, that way, it becomes more valuable. You can use Zoom for the interview. I used it also to make the professional interviews for the conferences.

4.) Written lecture materials:
If the first three is too hard for you yet, you can also make written lectures with downloadable PDF materials. There are topics where the form of the written text is excessively enough but unfortunately in most of the cases you have to make videos. Written courses are usually technically featured, such as programming.

What are you going to need while making the course?

You will be able to reach the greatest result if you use the best available price-ratio tools. Professional online courses consist of videos and downloadable PDF-s. These are supplemented by Facebook group membership but its main core is defined by short, video lessons.

1.) Video recording devices and the right location
You have to use videos in many places, and for this, you will only need your mobile phone and a little bit of encouragement. I have already made many courses and there are 4-5 screen video recordings in them where I instruct the participants and another 2-3 videos in which I personally welcome them. A personal video is needed as well because without it your course will be an incomprehensible flood of information. You must add some personal touch to it so that the participants will feel closer.

You can record the educational videos by using a screen recording or a presentation making software as well. Keynote and Powerpoint are also able to record presentation videos.

Location is also important. You can record your videos outside or in your office. The background can highlight the topic of your course as well as the expert image.

2.) Video editing software, audio and video effects
You can choose from among a tremendous amount of video editing software. There are some that works on your mobile or on tablet as well but the majority of them can be used only on a personal computer or on a laptop.

When you choose a software, you have to make a decision in advance about what you would like to use it for. If you just simply edit the video and you would not like to apply any impressive effect, it is enough to use simpler software.

Some of the video making software I recommend:
Online invideo application, Adobe Premier software, iMovie and Final Cut Pro on Mac but you can use Adobe Premiere Clip or Splice from GoPro as well.

3.)Landing pages and sales funnels
Basically, Wordpress can be enough with an Avada/Elementor or a DIVI topic. If you learn how to use this, you will be able to create nice and efficient landing pages. Another opportunity is a landing page creating software such as Instapage, Unbounce or Leadpages. The later one I also had used for a couple of years until Kajabi came out. Kajabi is also able to do all these, which means that it contains everything you need. You can create landing pages as well as websites with it + your online courses.

4.)Course platform where you can educate online
I recommend you two opportunities which both are the best choices in their own markets. The first solution is one that you pay for monthly, and it is quite a high price but in return, it can do anything you will ever need. The other one is free of charge basically but extension is needed for it and also a great topic that makes your work easy.

1.) Kajabi, the all-in-one Software:
Let's start with Kajabi, „the all-in-one software". It is worth knowing what Kajabi knows exactly and after that make an evaluation

regarding its price. I have been using this software since 2015 and I am satisfied with it as it is capable of anything I need. My courses are in a system that can be handled easily, I can send e-mail campaigns and I can make landing pages and sales funnels in an instant.

I recommend Kajabi to those who would not like to risk.

You receive everything from one single software that you need in order to build your business. Kajabi users are much more relaxed as they use one software that includes everything. In contrast, the basically free Wordpress means constant anxiety. The software becomes outdated, it can be hacked or many other annoying difficulties can occur.

Let's see what does Kajabi software consists of:

Products: You created your subscription system, your online courses and your digital products in the system of Kajabi. You can make professional online courses from a new idea even in minutes. It is a simple and an effective tool.

Websites: You can manage your website as well as your courses, your landing pages and everything that is part of your online course business.

CRM and Analytics: A professional CRM analytics is also part of the system that supports your decisions. You are able to send e-mails only to those who have not bought your course yet.

E-mail: You are also given a simple and effective e-mail marketing software with Kajabi: automated e-mail series, e-mail campaigns that can be done in seconds and a professional e-mail delivery statistics are also included.

Pipelines: You can create sales funnels simply and quickly by the help of pre-prepared funnels.

Mobile: You are also given a mobile application to the system. Your customers can complete your course on their mobile phones as well. You can offer the world's most comfortable educational materials.

Certainly, this is only a part of Kajabi system therefore I definitely recommend you to try it for free.

Free trial link: https://bit.ly/28napingyen

2.) Wordpress + Membermouse + DIVI :

Wordpress is free of charge and can be used really easily. I recommend it to those who do not possess such an amount of capital that would enable them to use the best software.

Wordpress+DIVI: Free of charge WordPress is not suitable alone for this function but a good topic (e.g.: Divi) can help to build up a website and a landing page which is featured by a modern design. It is going to be a lot of time and hard work to build such a quality as with Kajabi.

Membermouse: This is a software

This is a software that is charged monthly, and its monthly rental fee rises depending on the number of members/customers. It has to be linked to WP and this way you can deliver your course to customers.

I would not like to sell a pig in a poke, therefore I wrote down everything you need to know before making the decision. Kajabi delivers all the functions you will need.

Wordpress + Divi + Membermouse requires a lot of time because you have to learn the whole system. If you feel that you have a lot of time, go ahead and learn it. But if you would like to build systems fast/simply, Kajabi is the best choice for you.

5.) Let's Sell Your

Online Course

5.) Let's sell your online course

The previous chapters of the book helped you to plan and build your 1st online course and the million income "Knowledge Commerce" business. Now let's see how you can sell your courses effectively.

Make your irrefutable offer

Million income campaigns have one thing in common. In each one of them there is an irrefutable offer which cannot be refused. Now we are going to make your own irrefutable offer step by step.

1. STEP: Collect all the elements

Start thinking about what else you can offer to your customers added to your course. Write down all your ideas on a piece of white paper. You will have to choose from among these the elements which are the part of your irrefutable offer and which will then become the bump-offer or up-sell offer. Increase the value of your offer. Overfulfil the expectations of your customers and the great results will come.

What elements should you include in your offer?
- Ebook, blogpost, checklist or case study
- Video, video series, video course or LIVE video
- Audio material or even personal consultation

Write as many as you can and put a price tag on them so that the customer can see how much value she or he gets for a reasonable price.

2. STEP: Name and price the elements of the offer

You must find names to each of the elements that raise their interest and include a great promise. eg.: 10 tips how you can get rid of debt

You must make 8-10 items that should be diverse. (Audio + video and downloadable text files in the package). Name them and write the representative value next to them. It is not easy to price professionally but you need to find the price of the best conversion and in order to be able do that you will need to test a lot.

Here is an example:
- 5 week advanced yoga course (VALUE: $1.997)
- 101 yoga exercises video course (VALUE: $1.997)
- 1 hour refreshing yoga background music (VALUE: $297)
- 50x100 cm soft yoga mat (VALUE: $97)
- 7 interviews with national yoga teachers (VALUE 197)
- 90 day Let's Do Yoga Group membership (VALUE $297)
- 15 minutes personal consultation (VALUE $597)

If you add the ones above, it is going to be about $5.550 in total. The price of the original course is $1.997 so we give 2.5 times of this amount in this package. All the elements of the offer would come through in itself, therefore it can be a functioning package offer.

As for the above offer it can also work if you give a discount from its price and you offer the whole package for $1.997 which is the price of your course anyway.

3. STEPS: Use the remaining items

It is probable that you had already placed the best items into your main offer. I hope that there are still some attractive items remained on the white paper as they will be needed for the following:

Bump-Offer: Choose an item that represents a great value and place it to the bottom of the order sheet. It can also be requested by a single click and increase the value of the basket that way. One quarter of the customers will request your offer if it is fascinating enough.

Up-sell:
Offer another deal on a page right after the purchase. It can also be a package deal that contains exciting items. 1-10% of your customers will request this one as well independently from its price. I have already seen a $297 deal but the ones for $997 are not rare either. It works the best if you target 50-150% of the original price.

STEP 4: Testing and fine-tuning

Call your customers and ask them which item of the offer was that made him or her decide purchase your offer. Ask his or her opinion about the items that did not raise his or her interest. As you gathered 100 replies, analyze the ones that do not do well and exchange them with items that are more exciting. You must test and optimize your offer continuously so that you can increase your income without the increase of traffic on your website.

Goal → Strategy → Tactics → Daily tasks

The next step of selling your course is to make your campaign. We need to clarify something right in the beginning. You need to advertise the lead magnet and start with building the list. It can be followed by an offer and some of the subscribers will make a purchase.

1#What is going to be the aim of your campaign?
Define the primary aim of the campaign so that you will not lose focus while making it. Define its primary goal so that you will not lose focus while making the campaign. Write down what you would like to achieve and how much time you would like to spend on achieving it. eg.: In the year 2021 I am going to help 10.000 mother-to-be to get back in shape.

2#Define the strategy that you use to achieve your goal
While continuing the first example now you must write down what strategies you are going to use to reach your goal. eg. You start your YouTube channel and you help your followers by uploading 1 video per week. You build your private Facebook group and you provide constant help for the mother-to-be. The third strategy can be that you make a free course where they can join in the Coaching program that they then pay for.

3#Work out the steps of the tactics
The tactics here can be for instance that your make your own YouTube channel and you schedule the tasks in your diary in advance. You order the equipment required to make the videos and you start producing the entertaining/educating recordings. For each and every strategy you have to work out all the tactics as what you want to achieve would not be realized without them.

4# Daily tasks and TO DOs

This is already the definition of daily tasks which means you must write down your daily duties. You can make ad creatives, you write the text and embed the measuring code. These will make your goals a reality. If you build it up precisely, you will see that you get closer and closer to your goal.

Why is it so important to systematize your business?
The truth is that if you do not apply the above mentioned 4 steps, you will have a randomly developing business. You will not see where you make the mistakes and therefore you will not be able to correct it.

If you work out these steps in detail and you build your business consciously, the job will be easier and you can reach much greater results.

IMPORTANT INFORMATION. Any of the 4 steps above can be modified flexibly but do not change a product or a target audience completely just because the results do not come immediately.
Be patient, insist on the 4 steps and invest enough work, time and energy. Believe in your own business because it will work really and only then.

You can reach your goal much quicker if you see the way from the start right until the finish line. This system of the 4 steps will be your map to success that you need to follow even if you have a bad day and you are not in the mood of working on it.

The Next Step...

Try Kajabi software for free!

As an official affiliate partner of Kajabi, I can provide you a 28 days free trial.

Request it here: https://bit.ly/28napingyen

By typing in the link above you receive a free online course + you can use the Kajabi software for 28 days free of charge. That way you will have time to test the software and if you are smart, you can even start selling your course.

Would you like to work with me?

Request my FREE mini course:

www.knowledgecommercemillionaire.com/freecourse

You can find more useful information on my website:

www.knowledgecommercemillionaire.com